BLACK THEOLOGY
AND BLACK POWER

ALSO BY JAMES H. CONE

A Black Theology of Liberation
For My People: Black Theology and the Black Church
God of the Oppressed
My Soul Looks Back
Speaking the Truth: Ecumenism, Liberation, and Black Theology
The Spirituals and the Blues

BLACK THEOLOGY AND BLACK POWER

JAMES H. CONE

HarperSanFrancisco
A Division of HarperCollinsPublishers

Library of Congress Cataloging-in-Publication Data
Cone, James H.
    Black theology and Black power / James H. Cone.
      p.   cm.
    Reprint. Originally published: New York : Seabury Press, 1969.
    Bibliography: p.
    ISBN 0-06-254864-6
    1. Race relations—Religious aspects—Christianity.   2. Black theology.   3. Black power.   I. Title.
BT734.2.C6 1989
230'.08996073—dc20   89-15227
                                                 CIP

93   94   95   96   97   RRD   10   9   8   7   6

To Rose

Preface to the 1989 Edition

Black Theology and Black Power was a product of the Civil Rights and Black Power movements in America during the 1960s, reflecting both their strengths and weaknesses. As an example of their strengths, this book was my initial attempt to identify *liberation* as the heart of the Christian gospel and *blackness* as the primary mode of God's presence. I wanted to speak on behalf of the voiceless black masses in the name of Jesus whose gospel I believed had been greatly distorted by the preaching and theology of white churches.

Although Martin Luther King, Jr., and other civil rights activists did much to rescue the gospel from the heresy of white churches by demonstrating its life-giving power in the black freedom movement, they did not liberate Christianity from its cultural bondage to white, Euro-American values. Unfortunately, even African-American churches had deviated from their own liberating heritage through an uncritical imitation of the white denominations from which they separated. Thus, it was hard to distinguish between the theologies of white and black churches and the images of God and Jesus they used to express them. African-Americans, it seemed to me at the time, had assumed that, though whites did not treat them right, there was nothing wrong with whites' thinking about God.

It was the challenging and angry voice of Malcolm X that shook me out of my theological complacency. "Christianity is the white man's religion," he proclaimed, again and again, as he urged African-Americans to adopt a perspective on God that was derived from their own cultural history. He argued:

Brothers and sisters, the white man has brainwashed us black people to fasten our gaze upon a blond-haired, blue-eyed Jesus! We're worshiping a Jesus that doesn't even *look* like us! Oh, yes! . . . Now just think of this. The blond-haired, blue-eyed white man has taught you and me to worship a *white* Jesus, and to shout and sing and pray to this God that's *his* God, the white man's God. The white man has taught us to shout and sing and pray until we *die*, to wait until *death*, for some dreamy heaven-in-the-hereafter, when we're *dead*, while this white man has his milk and honey in the streets paved with golden dollars here on *this* earth!

Since I was, like many African-American ministers, a devout follower of Martin King, I tried initially to ignore Malcolm's cogent *cultural* critique of the Christianity as it was taught and practiced in black and white churches. I did not want him to disturb the theological certainties that I had learned in graduate school. But with the urban unrest in the cities and the rise of Black Power during the James Meredith March in Mississippi (June 1966), I could no longer ignore Malcolm's devastating criticisms of Christianity, particularly as they were being expressed in the articulate and passionate voices of Stokely Carmichael, Ron Karenga, the Black Panthers, and other young African-American activists. For me, the burning theological question was, how can I reconcile Christianity and Black Power, Martin Luther King, Jr.'s idea of nonviolence and Malcolm X's 'by any means necessary' philosophy? The writing of *Black Theology and Black Power* was the beginning of my search for a resolution of that dilemma.

Considered within the sociopolitical context of the sixties, I still believe that my answer was correct: "Christianity . . . is Black Power." Since theology is *human* speech and *not* God speaking, I recognize today, as I did then, that *all* attempts to speak about ultimate reality are limited by the social history of the speaker. Thus, I would not use exactly the same language today to speak about God that I used twenty years ago. Times have changed and the current situation demands a language appropriate for the problems we now face. But insofar as racism is still found in the churches and in society, theologians and preachers of the Christian gospel must make it unquestionably clear that the God of Moses and of Jesus makes an unqualified solidarity with the victims, empowering them to fight against injustice.

As in 1969, I unfortunately still see today that most white and black churches alike have lost their way, enslaved to their own bureaucracies—with the clergy and staff attending endless meetings and professional theologians reading learned papers to each other, seemingly for the exclusive purpose of advancing their professional careers. In view of the silence of the great majority of white theologians when faced with the realities of slavery and segregation, the white churches' preoccupation with "academic" issues in theology and their avoidance of the issue of justice, especially in the area of race, do not surprise me. What does surprise and sadden me, however, is a similar situation among many African-American churches and their theologians, especially those who claim to speak and act in the name of a black theology of liberation. In view of Sojourner Truth and Fannie Lou Hamer, Martin King and Malcolm X and the tradition of resistance that they and others like them embody, African-American ministers and theologians should know better than lose themselves in their own professional advancement, as their people, especially the youth, are being destroyed by drugs, street gangs, and AIDS. More black youth are in jails and prisons than in colleges and universities. Our community is under siege; something must be done before it is too late. If there is to be any genuine future for the black church and black theology, we African-American theologians and preachers must develop the courage to speak the truth about ourselves, saying to each other and to our church leaders what we have often said and still say to whites: *Enough is enough! It is time for this mess to stop!* Hopefully, the re-issuing of *Black Theology and Black Power* will contribute to the development of creative self-criticism in both black and white churches.

An example of the weakness of the 1960s black freedom movement, as defined by *Black Theology and Black Power,* was its complete blindness to the problem of sexism, especially in the black church community. When I read my book today, I am embarrassed by its sexist language and patriarchal perspective. There is not even one reference to a woman in the whole book! With black women playing such a dominant role in the African-American liberation struggle, past and present, how could I have been so blind?

The publication of the twentieth-anniversary edition tempted me to rid *Black Theology and Black Power* of its sexist language (as I did in the revised edition of *A Black Theology of Liberation* [Orbis, 1986] and also insert some references to black women. But I decided to let the language remain unchanged as a reminder of how sexist I once was and also that I might be encouraged never to forget it. It is easy to change the language of oppression without changing the sociopolitical situation of its victims. I know existentially what this means from the vantage point of racism. Whites have learned how to use less offensive language, but they have not changed the power relations between blacks and whites in the society. Because of the process of changing their language, combined with the token presence of middle-class African-Americans in their institutions, it is now even more difficult to define the racist behavior of whites.

The same kind of problem is beginning to emerge in regard to sexism. With the recent development of womanist theology, as expressed in the articulate and challenging voices of Delores

Williams, Jackie Grant, Katie Cannon, Renita Weems, Cherl Gilkes, Kelly Brown, and others, even African-American male ministers and theologians are learning how to talk less offensively about women's liberation. Many seem to have forgotten that they once used exclusive language. Amnesia is an enemy of justice. We must never forget what we once were lest we repeat our evil deeds in new forms. I do not want to forget that I was once silent about the oppression of women in the church and the society. Silence gives support to the powers that be. It is my hope that by speaking out against sexism other male African-American preachers and theologians, especially in the historic black churches, will also lift their prophetic voices against this enemy of God in the black church community. So far, too few of us have spoken out in our own denominations.

Black Theology and Black Power is also limited by the Western theological perspective that I was fighting against. After spending six years of studying white theology in graduate school, I knew that the time had come for me to make a decisive break with my theological mentors. But that was easier said than done. I did not know much about my own theological tradition which had given rise to my rebellion. I was struggling to become a black radical theologian without much knowledge of the historical development of African-American religion and radicalism. I had studied a little "Negro History" in high school and college, but no text by a black author had been included in my theological curriculum in graduate school. That was one of the things that made me so angry. I had been greatly miseducated in theology, and it showed in the neo-orthodox, Barthian perspective of Black Theology and Black Power.

"How can you call what you have written 'black theology,'" African-American theologians pointedly asked me, "when most of the theological sources you use to articulate your position are derived from the white theology you claim to be heretical?" "Your theology," they continued, "is black in name only and not in reality. To be black in the latter sense, you must derive the sources and the norm from the community in whose name you speak." That criticism was totally unexpected, and it shook me as nothing else had. I had expected my black brothers and sisters to support me in my attacks on white theology. But it seemed to me at the time that they were attacking me instead of our enemies. In time, however, I came to see the great value of their criticism. My effort to correct this cultural weakness in my theological perspective has been an on-going process since the publication of *The Spirituals and the Blues* (1972).

As I began to reflect more deeply upon my own cultural history, tracing it back to the African continent, I began to see the great limitations of Karl Barth's influence upon my Christological perspective. Barth's assertion of the Word of God in opposition to natural theology in the context of Germany during the 1930s may have been useful. But the same theological methodology cannot be applied to the cultural history of African-Americans in the Americas or to Africans and Asians on their continents. Of course, I knew that when I wrote *Black Theology and Black Power*, but my theological training in neo-orthodoxy hindered my ability to articulate this point.

As in 1969, I still regard Jesus Christ today as the chief focus of my perspective on God but not to the exclusion of other religious perspectives. God's reality is not bound by one manifestation of the divine in Jesus but can be found wherever people are being empowered to fight for freedom. Life-giving power for the poor and the oppressed is the primary criterion that we must use to judge the adequacy of our theology, not abstract concepts. As Malcolm X put it: "I believe in a religion that believes in freedom. Any time I have to accept a religion that won't let me fight a battle for my people, I say to hell with that religion."

 Another weakness of *Black Theology and Black Power* was my failure to link the African-American struggle for liberation in the United States with similar struggles in the Third World. If I had listened more carefully to Malcolm X and Martin King, I might have avoided that error. Both made it unquestionably clear, especially in their speeches against the U.S. government's involvement in the Congo and Vietnam, that there can be no freedom for African-Americans from racism in this country unless it is tied to the liberation of Third World nations from U.S. imperialism.

"You can't understand what is going on in Mississippi if you don't understand what is going in the Congo." Malcolm told a Harlem audience. "They're both the same. The same interests are at stake. The same sides are drawn up, the same schemes are at work in the Congo that are at work in Mississippi." During the last year of his life, Malcolm traveled throughout the Middle East and Africa as he sought to place the black freedom struggle in the United States into an international context. When African-American leaders questioned the value of his international focus, Malcolm said: "The point that I would like to impress upon every Afro-American leader is that there is no kind of action in this country ever going to bear fruit unless that action is tied in with the overall international struggle."

Martin King shared a similar concern. Against the advice of many friends in the civil rights movement, churches, and government, he refused to separate peace and civil rights issues. His condemnation of his government's involvement in the war in Vietnam, referring to "America as the greatest purveyor of violence in the world today," alienated many supporters in both the white and black communities. Martin King contended that the black freedom struggle and the struggle of the Vietnamese for self-determination were tied together because "injustice anywhere is a threat to justice everywhere."

My failure to link black liberation theology to the global struggles for freedom contributed to my blindness regarding the problem of classism. Class privilege was (and still is) a dominant reality in the white community of the United States as well as in the African-American community. In fact, the problem of oppression in the world today is defined not exclusively in terms of race but also in terms of the great economic gap between rich and poor nations and the haves and havenots within them. Again, if I had listened more attentively to Martin King and Malcolm X, I might have seen what I did not see at the time I wrote *Black Theology and Black Power*. Both turned toward economic issues during their later lives. They saw the great limitations of capitalism and, while rejecting the anti-democratic and atheistic principles of the Soviet Union, Martin and Malcolm began to search for the human, democratic side of socialism. What was clear to both of them, and clear to me now, is that we need to develop a struggle for freedom that moves beyond race to include all oppressed peoples of the world. As Malcolm X told a Columbia University audience a few days before his assassination: "It is incorrect to classify the revolt of the Negro as simply a racial conflict of black against white or as a purely American problem. Rather, we are today seeing a global rebellion of the oppressed against the oppressor, the exploited against the exploiter."

Despite its limitations, I hope that *Black Theology and Black Power* will remind all who read it that good theology is not abstract but concrete, not neutral but committed. Why? Because the poor were created for freedom and not for poverty.

James H. Cone
Charles A. Briggs Distinguished Professor
    of Systematic Theology
Union Theological Seminary, New York
February 1989

Preface

The appearance of this book is made possible by the assistance and encouragement of many people. Although I cannot mention all, I must express my gratitude to those persons who participated directly in the bringing of this work into existence. First of all, I wish to express my gratitude to the faculty of Colgate Rochester Divinity School for the invitation to deliver these lectures as a Theological Fellow, and to the Faculty Development Committee of Adrian College for the summer grant which provided some financial assistance during my writing.

I want to thank my brother, the Reverend Cecil W. Cone I, for providing me office space in his church and for his critical reading of the manuscript. Dr. William Hordern, my former teacher, also took time away from his busy schedule as president of Lutheran Theological Seminary, Saskatoon, to read the manuscript and to encourage me to seek its publication. I must express my gratitude to Don Ernst, my colleague at Adrian College, who also read the manuscript and suggested many helpful stylistic changes.

I am particularly indebted to Dr. Lester Scherer, my friend and colleague in the Religion Department, who read the manuscript and rendered invaluable editorial assistance. He spent many hours away from his responsibilities reading and discussing the book with me as we worked for the publication deadline.

It would be difficult to express adequately my appreciation to Dr. C. Eric Lincoln of Union Theological Seminary. His friendship and professional encouragement have been invaluable to me. Also special thanks must be rendered to Dr. Lincoln for bringing my manuscript to the attention of The Seabury Press.

My wife deserves a special word of thanks for her understanding patience and for meeting the typing deadline for the final draft. She also provided an atmosphere for my writing by being both mother and father to our sons, Michael and Charles, during my extended periods of absence.

Although many persons assisted me in this work, I alone am responsible for the ideas which are set forth.

CONTENTS

Introduction

"Black Power" is an emotionally charged term which can evoke either angry rejection or passionate acceptance. Some critics reject Black Power because to them it means blacks hating whites, while others describe it as the doctrine of Booker T. Washington in contemporary form.[1] But the advocates of Black Power hail it as the only viable option for black people. For these persons Black Power means black people taking the dominant role in determining the black-white relationship in American society.

If, as I believe, Black Power is the most important development in American life in this century, there is a need to begin to analyze it from a theological perspective. In this work an effort is made to investigate the concept of Black Power, placing primary emphasis on its relationship to Christianity, the Church, and contemporary American theology.

I know that some religionists would consider Black Power as the work of the Antichrist. Others would suggest that such a concept should be tolerated as an expression of Christian love to the misguided black brother. It is my thesis, however, that Black Power, even in its most radical expression, is not the antithesis of Christianity, nor is it a heretical idea to be tolerated with painful forbearance. It is, rather, Christ's central message to twentieth-century America. And unless the empirical denominational

1

church makes a determined effort to recapture the man Jesus through a total identification with the suffering poor as expressed in Black Power, that church will become exactly what Christ is not.

That most churches see an irreconcilable conflict between Christianity and Black Power is evidenced not only by the de facto segregated structure of their community, but by their typical response to riots: "I deplore the violence but sympathize with the reasons for the violence." Churchmen, laymen and ministers alike, apparently fail to recognize their contribution to the ghetto condition through permissive silence—except for a few resolutions which they usually pass once a year or immediately following a riot—and through their co-tenancy of a dehumanizing social structure whose existence depends on the continued enslavement of black people. If the Church is to remain faithful to its Lord, it must make a decisive break with the structure of this society by launching a vehement attack on the evils of racism in all forms. It must become *prophetic,* demanding a radical change in the interlocking structures of this society.

This work, then, is written with a definite attitude, the attitude of an angry black man, disgusted with the oppression of black people in America and with the scholarly demand to be "objective" about it. Too many people have died, and too many are on the edge of death. In fairness to my understanding of the truth, I cannot allow myself to engage in a dispassionate, noncommitted debate on the status of the black-white relations in America by assessing the pro and con of Black Power. The scholarly demand for this kind of "objectivity" has come to mean being uninvolved or not taking sides. But as Kenneth B. Clark reminds us, when

moral issues are at stake, noninvolvement and non-commitment and the exclusion of feeling are neither sophisticated nor objective, but naïve and violative of the scientific spirit at its best. When human feelings are part of the evidence, they cannot be ignored. Where anger is the appropriate response, to exclude the recognition and acceptance of anger, and even to avoid the feeling itself as if it were an inevitable contamination, is to set boundaries upon truth itself. If a scholar who studied Nazi concentration camps did not feel revolted by the evidence no one would say he was unobjective but rather fear for his sanity and moral sensitivity. Feeling may twist judgment, but the lack of it may twist it even more.[2]

The prophets certainly spoke in anger, and there is some evidence that Jesus got angry. It may be that the importance of any study in the area of morality or religion is determined in part by the emotion expressed. It seems that one weakness of most theological works is their "coolness" in the investigation of an idea. Is it not time for theologians to get upset?

To say that this book was written in anger and disgust (without denying "a certain dark joy") is to suggest that it is not written chiefly for black people. At least it is no handbook or collection of helpful hints on conducting a revolution. No one can advise another on when or how to die. This is a word to the oppressor, a word to Whitey, not in hope that he will listen (after King's death who can hope?) but in the expectation that my own existence will be clarified. If in this process of speaking for myself, I should happen to touch the souls of black brothers (including black men in white skins), so much the better. I believe that all aspiring black intellectuals share the task that LeRoi Jones has described for the black artist in America: "To aid in the destruction of America as he knows it."

His role is to report and reflect so precisely the nature of the society, that other men will be moved by the exactness of his rendering, and if they are black men, grow strong through this moving, having seen their own strength, and weakness, and if they are white men, tremble, curse, and go mad, because they will be drenched with the filth of their evil.[3]

I am critical of white America, because this is *my* country; and what is mine must not be spared my emotional and intellectual scrutiny. Although my motive for writing was not—did not dare to be—dependent upon the response of white people, I do not rule out the possibility of creative changes, even in the lives of oppressors. It is illegitimate to sit in judgment on another man, deciding how he will or must respond. That is another form of oppression.

I

Toward a Constructive
Definition of Black Power

> If there is no struggle, there is no progress. Those who
> profess to favor freedom, and yet depreciate agitation,
> are men who want crops without plowing up the ground. They
> want rain without thunder and lightning. . . . This struggle
> may be a moral one; or it may be a physical one; or it may be
> both moral and physical; but there must be a struggle.
>
> *Frederick Douglass*

What Is Black Power?

There has been and still is much debate among the critics of
Black Power regarding the precise meaning of the words. The
term "Black Power" was first used in the civil rights movement
in the spring of 1966 by Stokely Carmichael to designate the only
appropriate response to white racism.[1] Since that time many
critics have observed that there is no common agreement regarding its definition. In one sense this fact is not surprising, since
every new phenomenon passes through stages of development,
and the advocates of Black Power need time to define its many
implications. But in another sense, this criticism is surprising,
since every literate person knows that imprecision, the inability of
a word to describe accurately the object of reality to which it
points, is characteristic of all languages. The complexity of this

5

problem is evident in the development of modern analytical philosophy. We are still in the process of defining such terms as "democracy," "good," "evil," and many others. In fact the ability to probe for deeper meanings of words as they relate to various manifestations of reality is what makes the intellectual pursuit interesting and worthwhile.

But if communication is not to reach an impasse, there must be agreement on the general shape of the object to which a term points. Meaningful dialogue is possible because of man's ability to use words as symbols for the real. Without this, communication ceases to exist. For example, theologians and political scientists may disagree on what they would consider "fine points" regarding the precise meaning of Christianity and democracy, but there is an underlying agreement regarding their referents.

The same is true of the words "Black Power." To what "object" does it point? What does it mean when used by its advocates? It means *complete emancipation of black people from white oppression by whatever means black people deem necessary.* The methods may include selective buying, boycotting, marching, or even rebellion. Black Power means black freedom, black self-determination, wherein black people no longer view themselves as without human dignity but as men, human beings with the ability to carve out their own destiny. In short, as Stokely Carmichael would say, Black Power means T.C.B., Take Care of Business—black folk taking care of black folks' business, not on the terms of the oppressor, but on those of the oppressed.

Black Power is analogous to Albert Camus's understanding of the rebel. The rebel says No and Yes. He says No to conditions considered intolerable, and Yes to that "something within him which 'is worthwhile' . . . and which must be taken into consideration." [2] To say No means that the oppressor has overstepped his bounds, and that "there is a limit beyond which [he] shall not go." [3] It means that oppression can be endured no longer in the style that the oppressor takes for granted. To say No is to reject categorically "the humiliating orders of the master" and by so doing to affirm that something which is placed above everything else, including life itself. To say No means that death is preferable to life, if the latter is devoid of freedom. *"Better to die on one's feet than to live on one's knees."* [4] This is what Black Power means.

It is in this light that the slogan "Freedom Now" [5] ought to be interpreted. Like Camus's phrase, "All or Nothing," Freedom Now means that the slave is willing to risk death because "he considers these rights more important than himself. Therefore he is acting in the name of certain values which . . . he considers are common to himself and to all men." [6] That is what Henry Garnet had in mind when he said "rather *die freemen, than live to be slaves.*" [7] This is what Black Power means.

A further clarification of the meaning of Black Power may be found in Paul Tillich's analysis of "the courage to be," which is "the ethical act in which man affirms his being in spite of those elements of his existence which conflict with his essential self-affirmation." [8] Black Power, then, is a humanizing force because it is the black man's attempt to affirm his being, his attempt to be recognized as "Thou," in spite of the "other," [9] the white power which dehumanizes him. The structure of white society attempts to make "black being" into "nonbeing" or "nothingness." In existential philosophy, nonbeing is usually identified as that which threatens being; it is that ever-present possibility of the inability to affirm one's existence. The courage to be, then, is the courage to affirm one's being by striking out at the dehumanizing forces which threaten being. And, as Tillich goes on to say, "He who is not capable of a powerful self-affirmation in spite of the anxiety of non-being is forced into a weak, reduced self-affirmation." [10]

The rebellion in the cities, far from being an expression of the inhumanity of blacks, is an affirmation of their being despite the ever-present possibility of death. For the black man to accept the white society's appeal to wait or to be orderly is to affirm "something which is less than essential . . . being." [11] The black man prefers to die rather than surrender to some other value. The cry for death is, as Rollo May has noted, the "most mature

form of distinctly human behavior." [12] In fact, many existentialists point out that physical life itself "is not fully satisfying and
meaningful until one can consciously choose another value which
he holds more dear than life itself." [13] To be human is to find
something worth dying for. When the black man rebels at the risk
of death, he forces white society to look at him, to recognize him,
to take his being into account, to admit that he *is*. And in a structure that regulates behavior, recognition by the other is indispensable to one's being. As Franz Fanon says: "Man is human only
to the extent to which he tries to impose his existence on another
in order to be recognized by him." [14] And "he who is reluctant
to recognize me opposes me. In a savage struggle I am willing to
accept convulsions of death, invincible dissolutions, but also the
possibility of the impossible." [15]

Black Power, in short, is an *attitude,* an inward affirmation of
the essential worth of blackness. It means that the black man will
not be poisoned by the stereotypes that others have of him,
but will affirm from the depth of his soul: "Get used to me,
I am not getting used to anyone." [16] And "if the white man
challenges my humanity, I will impose my whole weight as a
man on his life and show him that I am not that 'sho good
eatin'' that he persists in imagining." [17] This is Black Power, the
power of the black man to say Yes to his own "black being,"
and to make the other accept him or be prepared for a struggle.

I find myself suddenly in the world and I recognize that I have one
right alone: That of demanding human behavior from the other.
One duty alone: That of not renouncing my freedom through my
choices.[18]

Black Power and Existential Absurdity

Before one can really understand the mood of Black Power,
it is necessary to describe a prior mood of the black man in a
white society. When he first awakens to his place in America and
feels sharply the absolute contradiction between *what is* and

what ought to be or recognizes the inconsistency between his view of himself as a man and America's description of him as a thing, his immediate reaction is a feeling of absurdity. The absurd

is basically that which man recognizes as the disparity between what he hopes for and what seems in fact to be. He yearns for some measure of happiness in an orderly, a rational and a reasonably predictable world; when he finds misery in a disorderly, an irrational and unpredictable world, he is oppressed by the absurdity of the disparity between the universe as he wishes it to be and as he sees it.[19]

This is what the black man feels in a white world.

There is no place in America where the black man can go for escape. In every section of the country there is still the feeling expressed by Langston Hughes:

> I swear to the Lord
> I still can't see
> Why Democracy means
> Everybody but me.

I can remember reading, as a child, the Declaration of Independence with a sense of identity with all men and with a sense of pride: "We hold these truths to be self-evident: that all men are created equal; that they are endowed by their creator with certain unalienable rights; that among them is life, liberty and the pursuit of happiness." But I also read in the Dred Scott decision, not with pride or identity, but with a feeling of inexplicable absurdity, that blacks are not human.

But it is too clear for dispute, that the enslaved African race were not intended to be included, and formed no part of the people who framed and adopted this declaration; for if the language, as understood in that day, would embrace them, the conduct of the distinguished men who framed the Declaration of Independence would have been utterly and flagrantly inconsistent with the principles they asserted; and instead of the sympathy of mankind . . . they would have deserved and received universal rebuke and reprobation.

Thus the black man *"had no rights which the white man was bound to respect."* [20]

But many whites would reply: "The Negro is no longer bought and sold as chattel. We changed his status after the Civil War. Now he is free." Whatever may have been the motives of Abraham Lincoln and other white Americans for launching the war, it certainly was not on behalf of black people. Lincoln was clear on this:

My paramount object in this struggle is to save the Union, and is not either to save or to destroy slavery. If I could save the Union without freeing any slave, I would do it; and if I could save it by freeing some and leaving others alone, I would also do that.[21]

If that quotation still leaves his motives unclear, here is another one which should remove all doubts regarding his thoughts about black people.

I will say then that I am not, nor ever have been in favor of bringing about in any way the social and political equality of the black and white races—that I am not nor ever have been in favor of making voters or jurors of Negroes, nor of qualifying them to hold office, nor to intermarry with white people; and I will say in addition to this that there is a physical difference between the white and black races which I believe will forbid the two races living together on terms of social and political equality. And inasmuch as they cannot so live, while they do remain together, there must be the position of superior and inferior, and I as much as any other man am in favor of having the superior position assigned to the white race.[22]

And certainly the history of the black-white relations in this country from the Civil War to the present unmistakably shows that as a people, America has never intended for blacks to be free. To this day, in the eyes of most white Americans, the black man remains subhuman.

Yet Americans continue to talk about brotherhood and equality. They say that this is "the land of the free and the home of the brave." They sing: My country 'tis of thee, sweet land of liberty." But they do not mean blacks. This is the black man's paradox, the absurdity of living in a world with "no rights which the white man [is] bound to respect."

It seems that white historians and political scientists have attempted, perhaps subconsciously, to camouflage the inhumanity of whites toward blacks.[23] But the evidence is clear for those who care to examine it. All aspects of this society have participated in the act of enslaving blacks, extinguishing Indians, and annihilating all who question white society's right to decide who is human.

I should point out here that most existentialists do not say that "man is absurd" or "the world is absurd." Rather, the absurdity arises as man confronts the world and looks for meaning. The same is true in regard to my analysis of the black man in a white society. It is not that the black man is absurd or that the white society as such is absurd. Absurdity arises as the black man seeks to understand his place in the white world. The black man does not view himself as absurd; he views himself as human. But as he meets the white world and its values, he is confronted with an almighty No and is defined as a thing. This produces the absurdity.

The crucial question, then, for the black man is, "How should I respond to a world which defines me as a nonperson?" That he is a person is beyond question, not debatable. But when he attempts to relate as a person, the world demands that he respond as a thing. In this existential absurdity, what should he do? Should he respond as he knows himself to be, or as the world defines him?

The response to this feeling of absurdity is determined by a man's ontological perspective. If one believes that this world is the extent of reality, he will either despair or rebel. According to Camus's *The Myth of Sisyphus,* suicide is the ultimate act of despair. Rebellion is epitomized in the person of Dr. Bernard Rieux in *The Plague.* Despite the overwhelming odds, Rieux fights against things as they are.

If, perchance, a man believes in God, and views this world as merely a pilgrimage to another world, he is likely to regard suffering as a necessity for entrance to the next world. Unfortunately Christianity has more often than not responded to evil in this manner.[24]

From this standpoint the response of Black Power is like Camus's view of the rebel. One who embraces Black Power does not despair and take suicide as an out, nor does he appeal to another world in order to relieve the pains of this one.[25] Rather, *he fights back with the whole of his being*. Black Power believes that blacks are not really human beings in white eyes, that they never have been and never will be, until blacks recognize the unsavory behavior of whites for what it is. Once this recognition takes place, they can make whites see them as humans. The man of Black Power will not rest until the oppressor recognizes him for what he is—man. He further knows that in this campaign for human dignity, freedom is not a gift but a right worth dying for.

Is Black Power a Form of Black Racism?

One of the most serious charges leveled against the advocates of Black Power is that they are *black* racists. Many well-intentioned persons have insisted that there must be another approach, one which will not cause so much hostility, not to mention rebellion. Therefore appeal is made to the patience of black people to keep their "cool" and not get too carried away by their feelings. These men argue that if any progress is to be made, it will be through a careful, rational approach to the subject. These people are deeply offended when black people refuse to listen and place such white liberals in the same category as the most adamant segregationists. They simply do not see that such reasoned appeals merely support the perpetuation of the ravaging of the black community. Black Power, in this respect, is by nature *irrational,* i.e., does not deny the role of rational reflection, but insists that human existence cannot be mechanized or put into neat boxes according to reason. Human reason though valuable is not absolute, because moral decisions—those decisions which deal with human dignity—cannot be made by using the abstract methods of science. Human emotions must be reckoned with. Consequently, black people must say No to all do-gooders who insist that they need more time. If such persons really knew oppression—knew it existentially in their guts—they would join black people in their fight for freedom and dignity. It is interesting that most people do understand why Jews can hate Germans. Why can they not understand why black people, who have been deliberately and systematically dehumanized or murdered by the structure of this society, hate white people? The general failure of Americans to make this connection suggests that the primary difficulty is their inability to see black men as men.

When Black Power advocates refuse to listen to their would-be liberators, they are charged with creating hatred among black people, thus making significant personal relationship between blacks and whites impossible. It should be obvious that the hate which black people feel toward whites is not due to the creation of the term "Black Power." Rather, it is a result of the deliberate and systematic ordering of society on the basis of racism, making black alienation not only possible but inevitable. For over three hundred years black people have been enslaved by the tentacles of American white power, tentacles that worm their way into the guts of their being and "invade the gray cells of their cortex." For three hundred years they have cried, waited, voted, marched, picketed, and boycotted, but whites still refuse to recognize their humanity. In light of this, attributing black anger to the call for Black Power is ridiculous, if not obscene. "To be a Negro in this country," says James Baldwin, "and to be relatively conscious is to be in rage almost all the time."

In spite of this it is misleading to suggest that hatred is essential to the definition of Black Power. As Camus says, "One envies what he does not have, while the rebel's aim is to defend what he is. He does not merely claim some good that he does not possess or of which he is deprived. His aim is to claim recognition for something which he has." [26] Therefore it is not the intention of the black man to repudiate his master's human dignity, but only his status as master.[27] The rebellion in the cities, it would seem, should not be interpreted as a few blacks who want something for nothing but as an assertion of the dignity of all black people. The black man is assuming that there is a common value which is recognizable by all as existing in all people, and he is testifying to that *something* in his rebellion. He is expressing his solidarity with the human race. With this in view, Camus's reinterpretation of the Cartesian formula, "I think, therefore I am," seems quite appropriate: "I rebel, therefore *we* exist."

It is important to make a further distinction here among black hatred, black racism, and Black Power. Black hatred is the black man's strong aversion to white society. No black man living in white America can escape it. Even a sensitive white man can say: "It is hard to imagine how any Negro American, no matter how well born or placed, can escape a deep sense of anger and a burning hatred of things white." [28] And another nonblack, Arnold Rose, is even more perceptive:

Negro hatred of white people is not pathological—far from it. It is a healthy human reaction to oppression, insult, and terror. White people are often surprised at the Negro's hatred of them, but it should not be surprising.

The whole world knows the Nazis murdered millions of Jews and can suspect that the remaining Jews are having some emotional reaction to that fact. Negroes, on the other hand, are either ignored or thought to be so subhuman that they have no feelings when one of their number is killed because he was a Negro. Probably no week goes by in the United States that some Negro is not severely beaten, and the news is reported in the Negro press. Every week or maybe twice a week almost the entire Negro population of the United States suffers an emotional recoil from some insult coming from the voice or pen of a leading white man. The surviving Jews had one, big, soul-wracking "incident" that wrenched them back to group identification. The surviving Negroes experience constant jolts that almost never let them forget for even an hour that they are Negroes. In this situation, hatred of whites and group identification are natural reactions.[29]

And James Baldwin was certainly expressing the spirit of black hatred when he said:

The brutality with which Negroes are treated in this country simply cannot be overstated, however unwilling white men may be to hear it. In the beginning—and neither can this be overstated—a Negro just cannot *believe* that white people are treating him as they do; he does not know what he has done to merit it. And when he realizes that the treatment accorded him has nothing to do with anything he has done, that the attempt of white people to destroy him—for that is what it is—is utterly gratuitous, it is not hard for him to think of white people as devils.[30]

This feeling should not be identified as black racism. Black racism is a myth created by whites to ease their guilt feelings. As long as whites can be assured that blacks are racists, they can find reasons to justify their own oppression of black people. This tactic seems to be a favorite device of white liberals who, intrigued by their own unselfish involvement in civil rights *for* the "Negro," like to pride themselves on their liberality toward blacks. White racists who are prepared to defend the outright subjugation of blacks need no such myth. The myth is needed by those who intend to keep things as they are, while pretending that things are in fact progressing. When confronted with the fact that the so-called progress is actually nonexistent, they can easily offer an explanation by pointing to the "white backlash" caused by "black racism."

But the charge of black racism cannot be reconciled with the facts. While it is true that blacks do hate whites, black hatred is not racism. Racism, according to Webster, is "the assumption that psychocultural traits and capacities are determined by biological race and that races differ decisively from one another, which is usually coupled with a belief in the inherent superiority of a particular race and its rights to dominance over others." Where are the examples among blacks in which they sought to assert their right to dominance over others because of a belief in black superiority? The only possible example would be the Black Muslims; and even here there is no effort of Black Muslims to enslave whites. Furthermore, if we were to designate them as black racists, they certainly are not dangerous in the same sense as white racists. The existence of the Black Muslims does not entitle whites to speak of black racism as a serious threat to the American society. They should be viewed as one possible and justifiable reaction to white racism. But in regard to Black Power, it is not comparable to white racism. Stokely Carmichael, responding to the charge of black supremacy, writes:

There is no analogy—by any stretch of definition or imagination— between the advocates of Black Power and white racists. . . . The goal of the racist is to keep black people on the bottom, arbitrarily and dictatorially as they have done in this country for over three hundred years. The goal of black self-determination and black self-identity—Black Power—is full participation in the decision making process affecting the lives of black people.[31]

Modern racism is European in origin, and America has been its vigorous offspring. It is the white man who has sought to dehumanize others because of his feelings of superiority or for his economic advantage. Racism is so embedded in this country that it is hard to imagine that any white man can escape it.

Black Power then is not black racism or black hatred. Simply stated, Black Power is an affirmation of the humanity of blacks in spite of white racism. It says that only blacks really know the extent of white oppression, and thus only blacks are prepared to risk all to be free. Therefore, Black Power seeks not understanding but conflict; addresses blacks and not whites; seeks to develop black support, but not white good will. Black

Power believes in the utter determination of blacks to be free and not in the good intentions of white society. It says: If blacks are liberated, it will be blacks themselves who will do the liberating, not whites.

Why Integration Is Not the Answer

Whites are not only bothered about "black racism" but also about the rejection of integration implied in Black Power. They say, "Now that we have decided to accept the Negro, he will have no part of it. You see, we knew he really preferred segregation." What, then, does Black Power say about integration?

One Black Power advocate, when a newsman asked, "What about integration?" responded, "Integration of what?" The implication is clear. If integration means accepting the white man's style, his values, or his religion, then the black man must refuse. There is nothing to integrate. The white man, in the very asking of the question, assumes that he has something which blacks want or should want, as if being close to white people enhances the humanity of blacks.[32] This question—What about integration?—also completely ignores the beastly behavior of the "devil white man" (Malcolm X's designation). Black people cannot accept relationship on this basis.

On the other hand, if integration means that each man meets the other on equal footing, with neither possessing the ability to assert the rightness of his style over the other, then mutual meaningful dialogue is possible. Biblically, this may be called the Kingdom of God. Men were not created for separation, and color is not the essence of man's humanity. But we are not living in what the New Testament called the consummated Kingdom, and even its partial manifestation is not too obvious. Therefore, black people cannot live according to what ought to be, but according to what *is*. To be sure, men ought to behave without color as the defining characteristic of their view of humanity, but they do not. Some men can verbally rise above color, but existentially they live according to it, sometimes without even being conscious of it. There are so few exceptions to this that the universal assertion is virtually untouched. Therefore, to ask blacks to act as if color does not exist, to be integrated into white society, is asking them to ignore both the history of white America and present realities. Laws may be passed, but only whites have the power to enforce them.

Instead, in order for the oppressed blacks to regain their identity, they must affirm the very characteristic which the oppressor ridicules—*blackness*. Until white America is able to accept the beauty of blackness ("Black is beautiful, baby"), there can be no peace, no integration in the higher sense. Black people must withdraw and form their own culture, their own way of life.

Integration, as commonly understood, is nothing but " 'a subterfuge for white supremacy'; i.e., as always involving only a token number of Negroes integrated into 'white institutions on the white man's terms.' " [33] As Professor Poussaint shows, this means blacks accepting the white man's view of himself, blacks saying, "Yes, [we are] inferior." [34]

Any careful assessment of the place of the black man in America must conclude that black self-hatred is the worst aspect of the legacy of slavery.[35] "The worst crime the white man has committed," writes Malcolm X, "has been to teach us to hate ourselves." During slavery, black people were treated as animals, and were systematically taught that such treatment was due them because of their blackness. "When slavery was abolished, the Negro had been stripped of his culture and left with this heritage: an oppressed black man in a white man's world." [36] When blacks were rewarded, it was because they behaved according to the stereotypes devised by whites. Coupled with this was the belief that "white is right" and "black is evil." Therefore, "lighter Negroes" were given better opportunities, while "darker Negroes" had doors closed to them, giving credence to the idea that the closer you are to being white, the more nearly human you are. Unfortunately, even many of our black institutions and media promoted the idea. As Elijah Muhammad, the leader of the Black Muslims, rightly says: "The Negro wants to be a white man. He processes his hair. Acts like a white man. He wants to integrate with the white man, but he cannot integrate with himself or his own mind. The Negro wants to lose his identity because he does not know his own identity."

In the present situation, while many of the mainline civil rights workers have promoted black identity by courageously fighting against an apparent, immovable status quo, the idea of integration, at this stage, too easily lends itself to supporting the moral superiority of white society.

Negro parents in the south never speak of sending their children to the "integrated school"; they say, "My child is going to the *white* school." No white children are "integrated" into Negro schools. Since integration is only a one-way street that Negroes travel to a white institution, then inherent in the situation itself is the implied inferiority of the black man.[37]

What is needed, then, is not "integration" but a sense of worth in being black, and only black people can teach that. Black consciousness is the key to the black man's emancipation from his distorted self-image.

As previously noted, some have called this racism in reverse. But this is merely a social myth, created by the white man to ease his guilt by accusing blacks of the same brutalities he has himself inflicted. The withdrawal of blacks is a necessary counterattack to overt, voluntary white racism. Furthermore, there is no way for blacks politically to enforce their attitudes, even if they were destructive of whites, but whites can and do enforce their attitudes upon blacks. Black identity is survival, while white racism is exploitation.

Black Power, then, must say No to whites who invite them to share in their inhumanity toward black people. Instead, it must affirm the beauty of blackness and by so doing free the black man for a self-affirmation of his own being as a black man. Whites cannot teach this.

Is There an Appropriate Response to White Racism?

The asking of this question is inevitable. Whites want to know whether Black Power is an appropriate response to their bigotry. It is indeed interesting that they, the oppressors, should ask this question, since whatever response blacks make is nothing but a survival reaction to white oppression. It is time for whites to realize that the oppressor is in no position whatever to define the proper response to enslavement. He is not the slave, but the enslaver. And if the slave should choose to risk death rather than submit to the humiliating orders of the master, then that is his right. Bigger Thomas in Richard Wright's *Native Son* demonstrates this choice when interrogated by white policemen who wanted him to confess raping a white girl:

"Come on, now, boy. We've treated you pretty nice, but we can get tough if we have to, see? It's up to *you!* Get over there by the bed and show us how you raped and murdered that girl!"

"I didn't rape her," Bigger said through stiff lips.

"Aw, come on. What you got to lose now? Show us what you did."

"I don't want to."

"You *have* to!"

"I *don't* have to."

"Well, we'll *make* you."

"You can't make me do nothing but die!" [38]

You can't make me do nothing but die! That is the key to an understanding of Black Power. Any advice from whites to blacks on how to deal with white oppression is automatically under suspicion as a clever device to further enslavement.

Furthermore, it is white intellectual arrogance which assumes that it has a monopoly on intelligence and moral judgment. How else can one explain the shocked indignation when the

Kerner Report declared that race prejudice has shaped our history decisively. After all, Baldwin, Wright, Du Bois, and a host of other black writers had been saying for decades that racism is woven into the whole pattern of American society. Evidently the judgments of black people are not to be taken seriously (if, indeed, Whitey reads them at all).

The real menace in white intellectual arrogance is the dangerous assumption that the structure that enslaves is the structure that will also decide *when* and *how* this slavery is to be abolished. The sociological and psychological reports, made by most white scholars, assume that they know more about *my* frustration, *my* despair, *my* hatred for white society than I do. They want to supply the prescriptions to my problems, refusing to recognize that for over three hundred years blacks have listened to them and their reports and we are still degraded. The time has come for white Americans to be silent and listen to black people. Why must the white man assume that he has the intellectual ability or the moral sensitivity to know what blacks feel or to ease the pain, to smooth the hurt, to eradicate the resentment? Since he knows that he raped our women, dehumanized our men, and made it inevitable that black children should hate their blackness, he ought to understand why blacks must cease listening to him in order to be free.

Since whites do not know the extent of black suffering, they can only speak from their own perspective, which they call "reason." This probably accounts for white appeals to nonviolence and Christian love. (The Christian understanding of love is discussed in Chapter II.) White people should not even expect blacks to love them, and to ask for it merely adds insult to injury. "For the white man," writes Malcolm X, "to ask the black man if he hates him is just like the rapist asking the *raped* . . . 'Do you hate me?' The white man is in no moral position to accuse anyone else of hate." Whatever blacks feel toward whites or whatever their response to white racism, it cannot be submitted to the judgments of white society.

When a white man asks, "Is Black Power the answer?" or says,

"It takes time," "Wait, let's talk it over and solve this problem together," "I feel the same way you do, but . . . ," I must conclude that he is talking from a different perspective. There is no way in the world I can get him to see that he is the problem, not me. He has shaped my response. Bennett, then, is right when he states:

We do not come up with the right answers to our problem because we seldom ask ourselves the right question. *There is no Negro problem in America; there has never been a Negro problem in America—the problem of race in America is a white problem.* To understand that problem and to control it, we must address ourselves to the fears and frailties of white people. We learn nothing really from a study of Harlem. To understand Harlem we must go not to Harlem but to the conscience of "good white people"; we must ask not what is Harlem but what have you made of Harlem? Why did you create it and why do you need it? [39]

Therefore, when blacks are confronted by whites who want to help with the "black problem" by giving advice on the appropriate response, whites should not be surprised if blacks respond, "We wish to plead our own cause. Too long have others spoken for us." [40] I am not prepared to talk seriously with a man who essentially says, "I sit on a man's back, choking him and making him carry me, and yet assure myself and others that I am very sorry for him and wish to lighten his load by all possible means —except by getting off his back." [41] Blacks must demand that whites get off their backs.

If whites do not get off the backs of blacks, they must expect that blacks will literally throw them off by whatever means are at their disposal. This is the meaning of Black Power. Depending on the response of whites, it means that emancipation may even have to take the form of outright rebellion. No one can really say what form the oppressed must take in relieving their oppression. But if blacks are pushed to the point of unendurable pain, with no option but a violent affirmation of their own being, then violence is to be expected. "Violence is a personal necessity for the oppressed," writes John Reilly in his analysis of Richard Wright's *Native Son*. "When life in a society consists of humiliation, one's only rescue is through rebellion. It is not a strategy consciously devised. It is the deep, instinctive expression of a human being denied individuality. . . . Yet expression of the rebellion can be liberating." [42] Or again, as Bennett says: "The boundary of freedom is man's power to say 'No!' and whoever refuses to say 'No' involves himself tragically in his own degradation." [43] Black Power says No!

How Does Black Power Relate to White Guilt?

When white do-gooders are confronted with the style of Black Power, realizing that black people really place them in the same category with the George Wallaces, they react defensively, saying, "It's not my fault" or "I am not responsible." Sometimes they continue by suggesting that their town (because of their unselfish involvement in civil rights) is better or less racist than others.

There are two things to be said here. First, there are no degrees of human freedom or human dignity. Either a man respects another as a person or he does not. To be sure, there may be different manifestations of inhumanity, but that is beside the point. The major question is: Is the black man in white society a "Thou" or an "It"? Fanon puts it this way: "A given society is racist or it is not. . . . Statements, for example, that the north of France is more racist than the south, that racism is the work of underlings and hence in no way involves the ruling class, that France is one of the less racist countries in the world are the product of men incapable of straight thinking." [44] Racism, then, biologically is analogous to pregnancy, either she is or she is not, or like the Christian doctrine of sin, one is or is not in sin. There are no meaningful "in betweens" relevant to the fact itself. And it should be said that racism is so embedded in the heart of American society that few, if any, whites can free themselves from it. So it is time for whites to recognize that fact for what it is and proceed from there. Who really can take it upon himself "to try to ascertain in what ways one kind of inhuman behavior differs from another,"[45] especially if one is a direct participant? "Is there in truth any difference between one racism and another? Do not all of them show the same collapse, the same bankruptcy of man?"[46]

Second, all white men are responsible for white oppression. It is much too easy to say, "Racism is not my fault," or "I am not responsible for the country's inhumanity to the black man." *The American white man has always had an easy conscience.* But insofar as white do-gooders tolerate and sponsor racism in their educational institutions, their political, economic, and social structures, their churches, and in every other aspect of American life, they are directly responsible for racism. "It is a cold, hard fact that the many flagrant forms of racial injustice North and South could not exist without their [whites'] acquiescence,"[47] and for that, they are responsible. If whites are honest in their analysis of the moral state of this society, they know that all are responsible. Racism is possible because whites are indifferent to suffering and patient with cruelty. Karl Jaspers' description of metaphysical guilt is pertinent here.

There exists among men, because they are men, a solidarity through which each shares responsibility for every injustice and every wrong committed in the world, and *especially for crimes that are committed in his presence or of which he cannot be ignorant.* If I do not do whatever I can to prevent them, I am an accomplice in them. If I have not risked my life in order to prevent the murder of other men, if I have stood silent, I feel guilty in a sense that cannot in any adequate fashion be understood juridically, or politically, or morally. . . . That I am still alive after such things have been done weighs on me as a guilt that cannot be expiated.[48]

In contrast, injustice anywhere strikes a sensitive note in the souls of black folk, because they know what it means to be treated as a thing. That is why Fanon says, "Anti-Semitism hits me head-on: I am enraged, I am bled white by an appalling battle, I am deprived of the possibility of being man. I cannot disassociate myself from the future that is proposed for my brother." [49] Yes, when blacks in Chicago hear about blacks being lynched in Mississippi, they are enraged. When they heard about Martin Luther King's death, they burned, they looted, they got Whitey. In fact, when blacks hear about any injustice, whether it is committed against black or white, blacks know that their existence is being stripped of its meaning. Aimé Césaire, a black poet, put it this way:

When I turn on my radio, when I hear that Negroes have been lynched in America, I say that we have been lied to: Hitler is not dead; when I turn on my radio, when I learn that Jews have been insulted, mistreated, persecuted, I say that we have been lied to: Hitler is not dead; when, finally I turn on my radio and hear that in Africa forced labor has been inaugurated and legalized, I say that we have been lied to: Hitler is not dead. [50]

White America's attempt to free itself of responsibility for the black man's inhuman condition is nothing but a protective device to ease her guilt. Whites have to convince themselves that they are not responsible. That is why social scientists prefer to remain detached in their investigations of racial injustice. It is less painful to be uninvolved. White Americans do not dare to know that blacks are beaten at will by policemen as a means of protecting the latter's ego superiority as well as that of the larger white middle class. For to know is to be responsible. To know is to understand why blacks loot and riot at what seems slight provocation. Therefore, they must have reports to explain the disenchantment of blacks with white democracy, so they can be surprised. They must believe that blacks are in poverty because they are lazy or because they are inferior. Yes, they must believe that everything is basically all right. Black Power punctures those fragile lies, declaring to white America the pitiless indictment of Francis Jeanson: "If you succeed in keeping yourself unsullied, it is because others dirty themselves in your place. *You hire thugs,* and, balancing the accounts, it is you who are

the real criminals: for without you, without your blind indifference, such men could never carry out deeds that damn you as
much as they shame those men." [51]

Black Power and the White Liberal

In time of war, men want to know who the enemy is. Who is
for me and who is against me? That is the question. The as-
serting of black freedom in America has always meant war.
When blacks retreat and accept their dehumanized place in
white society, the conflict ceases. But when blacks rise up in
freedom, whites show their racism.

In reality, then, *accommodation* or *protest* seems to be the
only option open to the black man. For three hundred years he
accommodated, thereby giving credence to his own enslavement.
Black Power means that he will no longer accommodate; that
he will no longer tolerate white excuses for enslavement; that
he will no longer be guided by the oppressor's understanding of
justice, liberty, freedom, or the methods to be used in attaining
them. He recognizes the difference between theoretical equality
and great factual inequalities. He will not sit by and wait for the
white man's love to be extended to his black brother. He will
protest, violently if need be, on behalf of absolute and immediate
emancipation. Black Power means that black people will cease
trying to articulate rationally the political advantages and moral
rightness of human freedom, since the dignity of man is a self-
evident religious, philosophical, and political *truth,* without which
human community is impossible. When one group breaks the
covenant of truth and assumes an exclusive role in defining the
basis of human relationship, that group plants the seed of rebellion. Black Power means that blacks are prepared to accept
the challenge and with it the necessity of distinguishing friends
from enemies.

It is in this situation that the liberal white is caught. We have
alluded to him earlier, but now we intend to take a closer look

at his "involvement" in this war for freedom. To be sure, as Loren Miller says, "there are liberals and liberals, ranging from Left to Right." But there are certain characteristics identifiable in terms of attitudes and beliefs.

Simply stated, [liberalism] contemplates the ultimate elimination of all racial distinctions in every phase of American life through an orderly, step-by-step process adjusted to resistance and aimed at overcoming such resistance. In the field of constitutional law, the classic liberal position, exemplified in the Supreme Court's "all deliberate speed" formula of school-segregation cases, requires and rationalizes Negro accommodation to, and acquiescence in, disabilities imposed because of race and in violation of the fundamental law.[52]

The liberal, then, is one who sees "both sides" of the issue and shies away from "extremism" in any form. He wants to change the heart of the racist without ceasing to be his friend; he wants progress without conflict. Therefore, when he sees blacks engaging in civil disobedience and demanding "Freedom Now," he is disturbed. Black people know who the enemy is, and they are forcing the liberal to take sides. But the liberal wants to be a friend, that is, enjoy the rights and privileges pertaining to whiteness and also work for the "Negro." He wants change without risk, victory without blood.

The liberal white man is a strange creature; he verbalizes the right things. He intellectualizes on the racial problem beautifully. He roundly denounces racists, conservatives, and the moderately liberal. Sometimes, in rare moments and behind closed doors, he will even defend Rap Brown or Stokely Carmichael. Or he may go so far as to make the statement: "I will let my daughter marry one," and this is supposed to be the absolute evidence that he is raceless.

But he is still white to the very core of his being. What he fails to realize is that there is no place for him in this war of survival. Blacks do not want his patronizing, condescending words of sympathy. They do not need his concern, his "love," his money. It is that which dehumanizes; it is that which enslaves. Freedom is what happens to a man on the inside; it is what happens to a man's being. It has nothing to do with voting, marching, picketing, or rioting—though all may be manifestations of it. No man can give me freedom or "help" me get it. A man is free when he can determine the style of his existence in an absurd world; a man is free when he sees himself for what he is and not as others define him. He is free when he determines the limits of his existence. And in this sense Sartre is right: "Man is freedom"; or, better yet, man "is condemned to be free." A man is free when he accepts the responsibility for his own acts and knows that they involve not merely himself but all men. No one can "give" or "help get" freedom in that sense.

In this picture the liberal can find no place. His favorite question when backed against the wall is "What can I do?" One is tempted to reply, as Malcolm X did to the white girl who asked the same question, "Nothing." What the liberal really means is, "What can I do and still receive the same privileges as other whites and—this is the key—be liked by Negroes?" Indeed the only answer is "Nothing." However, there are places in the Black Power picture for "radicals," that is, for men, white or black, who are prepared to risk life for freedom. There are places for the John Browns, men who hate evil and refuse to tolerate it anywhere.[53]

Black Power: Hope or Despair?

White racism is a disease. No excuse can be made for it; we blacks can only oppose it with every ounce of humanity we have. When black children die of rat bites, and black men suffer because meaning has been sapped from their existence, and black women weep because family stability is gone, how can anyone appeal to "reason"? Human life is at stake. In this regard black people are no different from other people. Men fight back, they grab for the last thread of hope. Black Power then is an expression of hope, not hope that whites will change the structure of oppression, but hope in the humanity of black people. If there is any expression of despair in Black Power, it is despair regarding white intentions, white promises to change the oppressive structure. Black people now know that freedom is not a gift from white society, but is, rather, the self-affirmation of one's existence as a person, a person with certain innate rights to say No and Yes, despite the consequences.

It is difficult for men who have not known suffering to understand this experience. That is why many concerned persons point out the futility of black rebellion by drawing a contrast between the present conditions of blacks in the ghetto and the circumstances of other revolutionaries in the past. The argument of these people runs like this: Revolutions depend on cohesion, discipline, stability, and the sense of a stake in society. The ghetto, by contrast, is relatively incohesive, unorganized, unstable, and numerically too small to be effective. Therefore, rebellion for the black man can only mean extermination, genocide. Moreover, fact one is that many poor blacks, being poor so long, have become accustomed to slavery, feeling any form of black rebellion is useless. And fact two, that the black bourgeoisie, having tasted the richness of white society, do not want to jeopardize their place in the structure.

This analysis is essentially correct. But to point out the futility of black rebellion is to miss the point. Black people know that they comprise less than 12 per cent of the total American population and are proportionately much weaker with respect to economic, political, and military power. And black radicals know that they represent a minority within the black community. But having tasted freedom through an identification with God's intention for humanity, they will stop at nothing in expressing their distaste for white power. To be sure, they may be the minority in the black community, but truth, despite democracy, can never be measured by numbers. Truth is that which places a man in touch with the real; and once a man finds it, he is prepared to give all for it. The rebellion in the cities, then, is not a conscious organized attempt of black people to take over; it is an attempt to say Yes to truth and No to untruth even in death. The question, then, is not whether black people are prepared to die—the riots testify to that—but whether whites are prepared to kill them. Unfortunately, it seems that that answer has been given through the riots as well. But this willingness of black people to die is not despair, it is hope, not in white people, but in their own dignity grounded in God himself. This willingness to die for human dignity is not novel. Indeed, it stands at the heart of Christianity.

II

The Gospel of Jesus,
Black People, and Black Power

One thing is clear. The damnation of the rich
is as lucid as the promise to the hungry.

Albert van den Heuvel

Contemporary theology from Karl Barth to Jürgen Moltmann conceives of the theological task as one which speaks from within the covenant community with the sole purpose of making the gospel meaningful to the times in which men live. While the gospel itself does not change, every generation is confronted with new problems, and the gospel must be brought to bear on them. Thus, the task of theology is to show what the changeless gospel means in each new situation.

On the American scene today, as yesterday, one problem stands out: the enslavement of black Americans. But as we examine what contemporary theologians are saying, we find that they are silent about the enslaved condition of black people. Evidently they see no relationship between black slavery and the Christian gospel.[1] Consequently there has been no sharp confrontation of the gospel with white racism. There is, then, a desperate need for a *black theology,* a theology whose sole purpose is to apply the freeing power of the gospel to black people under white oppression.

In more sophisticated terms this may be called a theology of revolution.[2] Lately there has been much talk about revolutionary theology, stemming primarily from non-Western religious thinkers whose identification lies with the indigenous oppressed people of the land.[3] These new theologians of the "Third World" argue that Christians should not shun violence but should initiate it, if violence is the only means of achieving the much needed rapid radical changes in life under dehumanizing systems. They are not confident, as most theologians from industrialized nations seem to be, that changes in the economic structure (from agrarian to industrial) of a country will lead to changes in its oppressive power-structure. (America seems to be the best indication that they are probably correct.) Therefore their first priority is to change the structures of power.

The present work seeks to be revolutionary in the sense that it attempts to bring to theology a special attitude permeated with black consciousness. It asks the question, What does the Christian gospel have to say to powerless black men whose existence is threatened daily by the insidious tentacles of white power? Is there a message from Christ to the countless number of blacks whose lives are smothered under white society? Unless theology can become "ghetto theology," a theology which speaks to black people, the gospel message has no promise of life for the black man—it is a lifeless message. Unfortunately, even black theologians have, more often than not, merely accepted the problems defined by white theologians. Their treatment of Christianity has been shaped by the dominant ethos of the culture. There have been very few, if any, radical, revolutionary approaches to the Christian gospel for oppressed blacks. There is, then, a need for a theology whose sole purpose is to emancipate the gospel from its "whiteness" so that blacks may be capable of making an honest self-affirmation through Jesus Christ.[4]

This work further seeks to be revolutionary in that "The fact that I am Black is my ultimate reality." [5] My identity with *blackness,* and what it means for millions living in a white world, controls the investigation. It is impossible for me to surrender this basic reality for a "higher, more universal" reality. Therefore, if a higher, Ultimate Reality is to have meaning, it must relate to the very essence of blackness. Certainly, white Western Christianity with its emphasis on individualism and capitalism as expressed in American Protestantism is unreal for blacks. And if Christianity is not real for blacks who are seeking black consciousness through the elements of Black Power, then they will reject it.

Unfortunately, Christianity came to the black man through white oppressors who demanded that he reject his concern for this world as well as his blackness and affirm the next world and whiteness. The black intellectual community, however, with its emphasis on black identity, is becoming increasingly suspicious of Christianity because the oppressor has used it as a means of stifling the oppressed concern for present inequities. Naturally, as the slave questions his existence as a slave, he also questions the religion of the enslaver. "We must," writes Maulana Ron Karenga, "concern ourselves more with this life which has its own problems. For the next life across Jordan is much further away from the growl of dogs and policemen and the pains of hunger and disease." [6]

Therefore, it is appropriate to ask: Is it possible for men to be *really* black and still feel any identity with the biblical tradition expressed in the Old and the New Testaments? Is it possible to strip the gospel as it has been interpreted of its "whiteness," so that its real message will become a live option for radical advocates of black consciousness? Is there any relationship at all between the work of God and the activity of the ghetto? Must black people be forced to deny their identity in order to embrace the Christian faith? [7] Finally, is Black Power, as described in Chapter I, compatible with the Christian faith, or are we dealing with two utterly divergent perspectives? These are hard questions. To answer these questions, however, we need to discuss, first, the gospel of Jesus as it relates to black people.

What Is the Gospel of Jesus?

Christianity begins and ends with the man Jesus—his life, death, and resurrection. He is the Revelation, the special disclosure of God to man, revealing who God is and what his purpose for man is. In short, Christ is the essence of Christianity. Schleiermacher was not far wrong when he said that "Christianity is essentially distinguished from other faiths by the fact that everything in it is related to the redemption accomplished by Jesus of Nazareth." [8] In contrast to many religions, Christianity revolves around a Person, without whom its existence ceases to be.

For this very reason Christology is made the point of departure in Karl Barth's *Church Dogmatics*. According to Barth, all theological talk about God, man, church, etc., must inevitably proceed from Jesus Christ, who is the sole criterion for every Christian utterance. To talk of God or of man without first talking about Jesus Christ is to engage in idle, abstract words which have no relation to the Christian experience of revelation. Therefore Barth is best known for his relentless, devastating attack on natural theology, which seeks knowledge of God through reason alone, independent of Jesus Christ. Whether one agrees with Barth or not regarding natural theology, he is at least right about what makes Christianity Christian. Wolfhart Pannenberg puts it this way:

All theological statements win their Christian character only through their connection with Jesus. It is precisely Christology that discusses and establishes the justification and the appropriate form of theological reference to Jesus in a methodological way. Therefore, theology can clarify its Christian self-understanding only by a thematic and comprehensive involvement with the Christological problems.[9]

Its teaching about Jesus Christ lies at the heart of every Christian theology.[10]

As Christians we know God only as he has been revealed in and through Jesus. All other talk about God can have, at most, provisional significance.[11]

One has only to read the gospel to be convinced of the central importance of Jesus Christ in the Christian faith. According to the New Testament, Jesus is the man for others who views his existence as inextricably tied to other men to the degree that his own Person is inexplicable apart from others. The others, of course, refer to all men, especially the oppressed, the unwanted of society, the "sinners." He is God himself coming into the very depths of human existence for the sole purpose of striking off the chains of slavery, thereby freeing man from ungodly principalities and powers that hinder his relationship with God. Jesus himself defines the nature of his ministry in these terms:

> The Spirit of the Lord is upon me,
> because he has anointed me to preach the good news to the poor.
> He has sent me to proclaim release to the captives
> and recovering of sight to the blind,
> To set at liberty those who are oppressed,
> To proclaim the acceptable year of the Lord.
>
> Luke 4:18–19, RSV

Jesus' work is essentially one of liberation. Becoming a slave himself, he opens realities of human existence formerly closed to man. Through an encounter with Jesus, man now knows the full meaning of God's action in history and man's place within it.

The Gospel of Mark describes the nature of Jesus' ministry in this manner: "The time is fulfilled, the Kingdom of God is at hand; repent and believe the Gospel" (1:14–15). On the face of it, this message appears not to be too radical to our twentieth-century ears, but this impression stems from our failure existentially to bridge the gap between modern man and biblical man. Indeed, the message of the Kingdom strikes at the very center of man's desire to define his own existence in the light of his own interest at the price of his brother's enslavement. It means the irruption of a new age, an age which has to do with God's action in history on behalf of man's salvation. It is an age of liberation, in which "the blind receive their sight, the lame walk, the lepers are cleansed, the deaf hear, the dead are raised up, the poor have the good news preached to them" (Luke 7:22). This is not pious talk, and one does not need a seminary degree to interpret the message. It is a message about the ghetto, and all other injustices done in the name of democracy and religion to further the social, political, and economic interests of the oppressor. In Christ, God enters human affairs and takes sides with the oppressed. Their suffering becomes his; their despair, divine despair. Through Christ the poor man is offered freedom now to rebel against that which makes him other than human.

It is ironical that America with its history of injustice to the poor (especially the black man and the Indian) prides itself as being a Christian nation. (Is there really such an animal?) It is even more ironic that officials within the body of the Church have passively and actively participated in these injustices. With Jesus, however, the poor were at the heart of his mission: "The last shall be first and the first last" (Matt. 20:16). That is why he was always kind to traitors, adulterers, and sinners and why the Samaritan in the parable came out on top. Speaking of Pharisees (the religious elite of his day), Jesus said: "Truly I say to you, the tax collectors [traitors] and harlots go into the kingdom—but not you" (Matt. 21:31).[12] Jesus had little toleration for the middle- or upper-class religious snob whose attitude attempted to usurp the sovereignty of God and destroy the dignity of the poor. The Kingdom is for the poor and not the rich because the former has nothing to expect from the world while the latter's entire existence is grounded in his commitment to worldly things. The poor man may expect everything from God, while the rich man may expect nothing because he refuses to free himself from his own pride. It is not that poverty is a precondition for entrance into the Kingdom. But those who recognize their utter dependence on God and wait on him despite the miserable absurdity of life are typically the poor, according to Jesus. And the Kingdom which the poor may enter is not merely an eschatological longing for escape to a transcendent reality, nor is it an inward serenity which eases unbearable suffering. Rather, it is God encountering man in the very depths of his being-in-the-world and releasing him from all human evils, like racism, which hold him captive. The repentant man knows that though God's ultimate Kingdom be in the future, yet even now it breaks through like a ray of light upon the darkness of the oppressed.

When black people begin to hear Jesus' message as contemporaneous with their life situation, they will quickly recognize what Jürgen Moltmann calls the "political hermeneutics of the gospel." Christianity becomes for them a religion of protest against the suffering and affliction of man.

One cannot grasp freedom in faith without hearing simultaneously the categorical imperative: One must serve through bodily, social and political obedience the liberation of the suffering creation out of real affliction. . . .

. . . Consequently, the missionary proclamation of the cross of the Resurrected One is not an opium of the people which intoxicates and incapacitates, but the ferment of new freedom. It leads to the awaking of that revolt which, in the "power of the resurrection" . . . follows the categorical imperative to overthrow all conditions in which man is a being who labors and is heavily laden.[13]

If the gospel of Christ, as Moltmann suggests, frees a man to be for those who labor and are heavily laden, the humiliated and abused, then it would seem that for twentieth-century America the message of Black Power is the message of Christ himself.

To be sure, that statement is both politically and religiously dangerous; politically, because Black Power threatens the very structure of the American way of life; theologically, because it may appear to overlook Barth's early emphasis on "the infinite qualitative distinction between God and man." In this regard, we must say that Christ never promised political security but the opposite; and Karl Barth was mainly concerned with the easy identification of the work of God with the work of the state. But if Luther's statement, "We are Christ to the neighbor," is to be taken seriously, and, if we can believe the New Testament witness which proclaims Jesus as resurrected and thus active even now, then he must be alive in those very men who are struggling in the midst of misery and humiliation. If the gospel is a gospel of liberation for the oppressed, then Jesus is where the oppressed are and continues his work of liberation there. Jesus is not safely confined in the first century. He is our contemporary, proclaiming release to the captives and rebelling against all who silently accept the structures of injustice. If he is not in the ghetto, if he is not where men are living at the brink of existence, but is, rather, in the easy life of the suburbs, then the gospel is a lie. The opposite, however, is the case. Christianity is not alien to Black Power; it is Black Power.

There are secular interpretations which attempt to account for the present black rebellion, as there have been secular interpretations of the exodus or of the life and death of Jesus. But for the Christian, there is only one interpretation: Black rebellion is a manifestation of God himself actively involved in the present-day affairs of men for the purpose of liberating a people. Through his work, black people now know that there is something more important than life itself. They can afford to be indifferent toward death, because life devoid of freedom is not worth living. They can now sing with a sense of triumph, "Oh, Freedom! Oh, Freedom! Oh Freedom over me! An' befo' I'd be a slave, I'd be buried in my grave, an' go home to my Lord an' be free."

Christ, Black Power, and Freedom

An even more radical understanding of the relationship of the gospel to Black Power is found in the concept of freedom. We have seen that freedom stands at the center of the black man's yearning in America. "Freedom Now" has been and still is the echoing slogan of all civil rights groups. The same concept of freedom is presently expressed among Black Power advocates by such phrases as "self-determination" and "self-identity."

What is this freedom for which blacks have marched, boycotted, picketed, and rebelled in order to achieve? Simply stated, freedom is *not doing what I will but becoming what I should.*[14] *A man is free when he sees clearly the fulfillment of his being and is thus capable of making the envisioned self a reality.* This is "Black Power!" They want the grip of white power removed what black people have in mind when they cry, "Freedom Now!" now and forever.

Is this not why God became man in Jesus Christ so that man might become what he is? Is not this at least a part of what St. Paul had in mind when he said, "For freedom, Christ has set us free" (Gal. 5:1)? As long as man is a slave to another power, he is not free to serve God with mature responsibility. He is not free to become what he is—human.

Freedom is indeed what distinguishes man from animals and plants. "In the case of animals and plants nature not only appoints the destiny but it alone carries it out. . . . In the case of man, however, nature provides only the destiny and leaves it to him to carry it out."[15] Black Power means black people carrying out their own destiny.

It would seem that Black Power and Christianity have this in common: the liberation of man! If the work of Christ is that of liberating men from alien loyalties, and if racism is, as George Kelsey says, an alien faith, then there must be some correlation between Black Power and Christianity. For the gospel proclaims that God is with us now, actively fighting the forces which would make man captive. And it is the task of theology and the Church to know where God is at work so that we can join him in this fight against evil. In America we know where the evil is. We know that men are shot and lynched. We know that men are crammed into ghettos. Black Power is the power to say No; it is the power of blacks to refuse to cooperate in their own dehumanization. If blacks can trust the message of Christ, if they can take him at his word, this power to say No to white power and domination is derived from him.

Looking at the New Testament, the message of the gospel is clear: Christ came into the world in order to destroy the works of Satan (I John 3:8). His whole life was a deliberate offensive against those powers which held man captive. At the beginning of his ministry there was a conflict with Satan in the wilderness (Luke 4:1–13; Mark 1:12ff.; Matt. 4:1–11), and this conflict continued throughout his ministry. In fact, every exorcism was a binding and despoiling of the evil one (Mark 3:27). It was not until Christ's death on the cross that the decisive battle was fought and won by the Son of man. In that event, the tyranny of Satan, in principle, came to an end. The Good News is that God in Christ has freed us; we need no longer be enslaved by alien forces. The battle was fought and won on Good Friday and the triumph was revealed to men at Easter.

Though the decisive battle against evil has been fought and won, the war, however, is not over. Men of the new age know that they are free, but they must never lose sight of the tension between the "now" and the "not yet" which characterizes this present age (II Tim. 1:10; Eph. 1:22; Heb. 2:8, 10:13). The crucial battle has been won already on the cross, but the campaign is not over. There is a constant battle between Christ and Satan, and it is going on now.

If we make this message contemporaneous with our own life situation, what does Christ's defeat of Satan mean for us? There is no need here to get bogged down with quaint personifications of Satan. Men are controlled by evil powers that would make them slaves. The demonic forces of racism are *real* for the black man. Theologically, Malcolm X was not far wrong when he called the white man "the devil." The white structure of this American society, personified in every racist, must be at least part of what the New Testament meant by the demonic forces. According to the New Testament, these powers can get hold of a man's total being and can control his life to such a degree that he is incapable of distinguishing himself from the alien power. This seems to be what has happened to white racism in America. It is a part of the spirit of the age, the ethos of the culture, so embedded in the social, economic, and political structure that white society is incapable of knowing its destructive nature. There is only one response: Fight it!

Moreover, it seems to me that it is quite obvious who is actually engaged in the task of liberating black people from the power of white racism, even at the expense of their lives. They are men who stand unafraid of the structures of white racism. They are men who risk their lives for the inner freedom of others. They are men who embody the spirit of Black Power. And if Christ is present today actively risking all for the freedom of man, he must be acting through the most radical elements of Black Power.

Ironically, and this is what white society also fails to understand, the man who enslaves another enslaves himself. Unrestricted freedom is a form of slavery. To be "free" to do what I will in relation to another is to be in bondage to the law of least resistance. This is the bondage of racism. Racism is that bondage in which whites are free to beat, rape, or kill blacks. About thirty years ago it was quite acceptable to lynch a black man by hanging him from a tree; but today whites destroy him by crowding him into the ghetto and letting filth and despair put the final touches on death. Whites are thus enslaved to their own egos. Therefore, when blacks assert their freedom in self-determination, whites too are liberated.[16] They must now confront the black man as a person.

In our analysis of freedom, we should not forget what many existentialists call the burden of freedom. Authentic freedom has nothing to do with the rugged individualism of *laissez faire*, the right of the businessman to pursue without restraint the profit motive or the pleasure principle which is extolled by Western capitalistic democracies. On the contrary, authentic freedom is grounded in the awareness of the universal finality of man and the agonizing responsibility of choosing between perplexing alternatives regarding his existence.

Therefore, freedom cannot be taken for granted. A life of freedom is not the easy or happy way of life. That is why Sartre says man "is condemned to freedom." Freedom is not a trivial birthday remembrance but, in the words of Dostoevsky's Grand Inquisitor, "a terrible gift." It is not merely an opportunity but a temptation. Whether or not we agree with the existentialists' tendency to make man totally autonomous, they are right in their emphasis on the burden of freedom.

In the New Testament, the burden of freedom is described in terms of being free from the law. To be free in Christ means that man is stripped of the law as a guarantee of salvation and is placed in a free, mature love-relationship with God and man, which is man's destiny and in which Christ is the pioneer. Christian freedom means being a slave for Christ in order to do his will. Again this is no easy life; it is a life of suffering because the world and Christ are in constant conflict. To be free in Christ is to be against the world.

With reference, then, to freedom in Christ, three assertions about Black Power can be made: First, the work of Christ is essentially a liberating work, directed toward and by the oppressed. Black Power embraces that very task. Second, Christ in liberating the wretched of the earth also liberates those responsible for the wretchedness. The oppressor is also freed of his peculiar demons. Black Power in shouting Yes to black humanness and No to white oppression is exorcizing demons on both sides of the conflict. Third, mature freedom is burdensome and risky, producing anxiety and conflict for free men and for the brittle structures they challenge. The call for Black Power is precisely the call to shoulder the burden of liberty in Christ, risking everything to live not as slaves but as free men.

The Righteousness of God and Black Power

To demand freedom is to demand justice. When there is no justice in the land, a man's freedom is threatened. Freedom and justice are interdependent. When a man has no protection under the law, it is difficult for him to make others recognize him, and thus his freedom to be a "Thou" is placed in jeopardy. Therefore it is understandable that freedom and justice are probably the most often repeated words when the black man is asked, "What do you want?" The answer is simple, freedom and justice—no more and no less.

Unfortunately, many whites pretend that they do not understand what the black man is demanding. Theologians and churchmen have been of little help in this matter because much of their intellectualizing has gone into analyzing the idea of God's righteousness in a fashion far removed from the daily experiences of men. They fail to give proper emphasis to another equally if not more important concern, namely, the biblical idea of God's righteousness as the divine decision to vindicate the poor, the needy, and the helpless in society. It seems that much of this abstract theological disputation and speculation—the favorite pastime for many theological societies—serves as a substitute for relevant involvement in a world where men die for lack of political justice. A black theologian wants to know what the gospel has to say to a man who is jobless and cannot get work to support his family because the society is unjust. He wants to know what is God's Word to the countless black boys and girls who are fatherless and motherless because white society decreed that blacks have no rights. Unless there is a word from Christ to the helpless, then why should they respond to him? How do we relate the gospel of Christ to people whose daily existence is one of hunger or even worse, despair? Or do we simply refer them to the next world?

The key to the answer, in the thinking of the black theologian, is in the biblical concept of the righteousness of God. According to the Bible, God and not man is the author of justice; and since justice is a part of the Being of God, he is bound to do justly. Whatever God does must be *just* because he is justice.

It is important to note that God's righteousness refers not so much to an abstract quality related to his Being in the realm of thought—as commonly found in Greek philosophy—but to his activity in human history, in the historical events of the time and effecting his purpose despite those who oppose it. This is the biblical tradition. Israel as a people initially came to know God through the exodus. It was Yahweh who emancipated her from Egyptian bondage and subsequently established a covenant with her at Sinai, promising: "You have seen what *I did* to the Egyptians, and how I bore you on eagles' wings and brought you to myself. Now therefore, if you will obey my voice and keep my covenant, you shall be my own possession among all peoples; . . . You shall be to me a kingdom of priests and a holy nation" (Exod. 19:4–6). Divine righteousness means that God will be faithful to his promise, that his purposes for Israel will not be thwarted. Israel, therefore, need not worry about her weakness and powerlessness in a world of mighty military powers, "for all the earth is mine" (Exod. 19:5). The righteousness of God means that he will protect her from the ungodly menacing of other nations. Righteousness means God is doing justice, that he is putting right what men have made wrong.

It is significant to note the condition of the people to whom God chose to reveal his righteousness. God elected to be the Helper and Saviour to people oppressed and powerless in contrast to the proud and mighty nations. It is also equally important to notice that within Israel, his righteousness is on behalf of the poor, defenseless, and unwanted. "If God is going to see

righteousness established in the land, he himself must be particularly active as 'the helper of the fatherless' (Ps. 10:14) to
'deliver the needy when he crieth; and the poor that hath no
helper' (Ps. 72:12)." [17] His vindication is for the poor because
they are defenseless before the wicked and powerful. "For this
reason," writes Barth, "in the relations and events in the life of
his people, God always takes his stand unconditionally and
passionately on this side alone: against the lofty and on behalf
of the lowly; against those who already enjoy right and privilege and on behalf of those who are denied it and deprived of
it." [18] This is certainly the message of the eighth-century prophets—Amos, Hosea, Isaiah, and Micah. Being ethical prophets,
concerned with social justice, they proclaimed Yahweh's intoler-
ance with the rich, who, as Amos says, "trample the head of
the poor into the dust of the earth" (2:7) and "sell the righteous
for silver, and the needy for a pair of shoes" (2:6). God unquestionably will vindicate the poor.

And if we can trust the New Testament, God became man
in Jesus Christ in order that the poor might have the gospel
preached to them; that the poor might have the Kingdom of
God (Luke 6:20); that those who hunger might be satisfied;
that those who weep might laugh.

If God is to be true to himself, his righteousness must be
directed to the helpless and the poor, those who can expect no
security from this world. The rich, the secure, the suburbanite
can have no part of God's righteousness because of their trust
and dependence on the things of this world. "God's righteousness triumphs when man has no means of triumphing." [19] His
righteousness is reserved for those who come empty-handed,
without any economic, political, or social power. That is why the
prophets and Jesus were so critical of the economically secure.
Their security gets in the way of absolute faith in God. "Earthly
possessions dazzle our eyes and delude us into thinking that
they can provide security and freedom from anxiety. Yet all the
time they are the very source of all anxiety." [20]

What, then, is God's Word of righteousness to the poor and the helpless? "I became poor in Christ in order that man may not be poor. I am in the ghetto where rats and disease threaten the very existence of my people, and they can be assured that I have not forgotten my promise to them. *My righteousness will vindicate your suffering!* Remember, I know the meaning of rejection because in Christ I was rejected; the meaning of physical pain because I was crucified; the meaning of death because I died. But my resurrection in Christ means that alien powers cannot keep you from the full meaning of life's existence as found in Christ. Even now the Kingdom is available to you. Even now I am present with you because your suffering is my suffering, and I will not let the wicked triumph." This is God's Word.

Those who wish to share in this divine righteousness must become poor without any possibility of procuring right for themselves. "The righteousness of the believer consists in the fact that God acts for him—utterly, because he cannot plead his own case and no one else can represent him." [21] The men of faith come to God because they can go to no one else. He, and he alone, is their security.

It is within this context that men should be reminded of the awesome political responsibility which follows from justification by faith. To be made righteous through Christ places a man in the situation where he too, like Christ, must be for the poor, for God, and against the world. As Barth puts it:

. . . there follows from this character of faith a political attitude, decisively determined by the fact that man is made responsible to all those who are poor and wretched in his eyes, that he is summoned on his part to espouse the cause of those who suffer wrong. Why? Because in them it is manifested to him what he himself is in the sight of God; because the living, gracious, merciful action of God towards him consists in the fact that God himself in his own righteousness procures right for him, the poor and wretched; because he and all men stand in the presence of God as those for whom right can be procured only by God himself. The man who lives by the faith that this is true stands under a political responsibility.[22]

No Christian can evade this responsibility. He cannot say that the poor are in poverty because they will not work, or they suffer because they are lazy. Having come before God as nothing and being received by him into his Kingdom through grace, the Christian should know that he has been made righteous (justified) so that he can join God in the fight for justice. Therefore, whoever fights for the poor, fights for God; whoever risks his life for the helpless and unwanted, risks his life for God. God is active now in the lives of those men who feel an absolute identification with all who suffer because there is no justice in the land.

Christian Love and Black Power

To suggest that Black Power is doing God's work in history by righting the wrongs done against his people will, of course, provoke the response that Black Power is a contradiction of Christian love. Critics will say: Even if Black Power is not hate, but as you say "self-determination by whatever means necessary —violence if need be," how can this be reconciled with the life and message of Jesus? Is not this a radical denial of his demand of love in which the power of God is expressed in weakness and humiliation?

These difficult questions should not be evaded since many Black Power advocates shun Christianity and the language of love. Nor do we adequately meet these questions by suggesting that Christianity with its emphasis on love is rejected because it is the oppressor's religion, though this is undoubtedly true. And even more specifically, critics will force us with the question: Is it not true that Black Power emerged because blacks became disenchanted with Martin Luther King's emphasis on Jesus' demand to *love* the enemy? "Martin King," says one Black Power advocate, "was trying to get us to love the white

folks before we learn to love ourselves, and that ain't no good." [23]
And another defines the problem in this manner:

> Too much love,
> Too much love,
> Nothing kills a nigger like
> Too much love.[24]

While most Black Power advocates do not prescribe hatred
(only a small minority), few, it must be admitted, would suggest love as the black man's appropriate response to white oppression. Most seem to feel like Malcolm X: "It's not possible
to love a man whose chief purpose in life is to humiliate you
and still be what is considered a normal human being." Therefore, instead of loving or hating the white man, it is best to
ignore him. "The white man no longer exists," writes one advocate. "He is not to be lived with and he is not to be destroyed.
He is simply to be ignored." [25]

Even a sympathetic admirer like Vincent Harding wonders
whether Black Power is actually participating in the same game
of dehumanization which it ascribes to white power. He pointedly asks: "What shall be said of a love that is willed toward
some men and not toward others? Is this goal in any way related to the deadly disease that has afflicted so much of American life for so many generations?" [26]

I certainly have no desire to make Christians out of those who
see no relationship between their understanding of truth and
Jesus Christ. It is not my thesis that all Black Power advocates
are Christians or even wish to be so. Nor is it my purpose to
twist their language or to make an alien interpretation of it.
My concern is, rather, to show that the goal and message of
Black Power, as defined in Chapter I and articulated by many
of its advocates, is consistent with the gospel of Jesus Christ.
Indeed, I have even suggested that if Christ is present among
the oppressed, as he promised, he must be working through the
activity of Black Power. This alone is my thesis. How then is it

possible to reconcile Black Power, and its emphasis on emancipation at all costs, with Christ's message of love?

In an attempt to answer that question, we must remember that it is most difficult to make first-century New Testament language relevant to a contemporary "world come of age." Jesus did not give us a blueprint for identifying God and his work or for relevant human involvement in the world. But this is the never-ending task of theology and the Church. The real temptation is to identify our own interest with God's and thus say that he is active in those activities which best serve our purposes. Karl Barth pointed out this danger in a convincing way in his *Romans* commentary. But we must speak of God and his work, if we intend to join him.

Our chief difficulty in coping with the relationship between Black Power and Christian love arises from the theological failure to interpret the New Testament message of salvation in such a way that it will have meaning for oppressed blacks in America. We still use, for the most part, traditional religious language which really was created for a different age and, to a large degree, for the Western white society. The New Testament message of God's love to man is still embedded in thought-forms totally alien to blacks whose life experiences are unique to themselves. The message is presented to blacks as if they shared the white cultural tradition. We still talk of salvation in white terms, love with a Western perspective, and thus never ask the question, What are the theological implications of God's love for the black man in America? Therefore when we are confronted with blacks with a new sense of themselves, alien to the Western definition of the black man and, to some degree, even alien to the Western view of humanity, our language seems to fail us as an attempt is made to "fit him in."

I am not suggesting that the New Testament language and its theological interpretation in the history of Western Christianity are no longer useful for black people in America. Rather, I am saying that there is a real need for a radical approach which takes the suffering of black people seriously. Without this new way of doing theology from the perspective of black enslavement, there will always be this barrier between Black Power and Christian love. This can be illustrated in the New Testament understanding of God's love for man and man's love for God and neighbor.[27]

According to the New Testament, man's love for God and for his neighbor is grounded in God's love for man, which most theologians designate as *agape*. God's agape to man is spontaneous and creative, the starting point of the God-man relationship.[28] It is spontaneous in that there is no worth in man from God's perspective which accounts for God's love. The sole reason for God's love is found in his loving character. As Nygren says: "Just by the fact that it [God's love] seeks sinners, who do not deserve it and can lay no claim to it, it manifests most clearly its spontaneous and unmotivated nature."[29] God's love is creative because "God does not love that which is already worthy of love, but on the contrary, that which in itself has no worth acquires worth just by becoming the object of God's love."[30] Thus, while all men are worthless apart from God's love, since God's love is bestowed upon all, all are worthy simply because God loves them. Herein lies the religious foundation for the equality of men. To suggest that some are worthy and some are not, or that "some are more equal than others" would mean that man has worth independent of God or that God's love is more creative in some than in others. As Nygren says: "Agape does not recognize value, but creates it. Agape loves and imparts value by loving. The man who is loved by God has no value in himself; what gives him value is precisely the fact that God loves him."[31]

God's love is the initiator of the God-man fellowship in that there is no way from man to God independent of agape. Because of God's act of love to man, man can now have fellowship with him. This is certainly demonstrated in God's election of Israel and his becoming man in Jesus Christ. In fact, everything that Christians mean by God's love is expressed in the Christ-event (John 3:16; Rom. 5:8). It is the man Jesus who "reveals God's love by what he says, does and is." [32] Like God's righteousness, his love is expressed in terms of his activity to and for man, which is the very basis of man's response to God and to his neighbor.

This activity of divine agape-love cannot be easily separated from God's righteousness. Indeed they must be held tightly together. Love prevents righteousness from being legalistic, and righteousness keeps love from being sentimental. Both express God's desire to be for man when man will not be for himself. Love means that God rights the wrongs of humanity because they are inconsistent with his purpose for man. Righteousness means that God cannot turn his back on evil, that he cannot pretend that wrong is right. Love means that he acts for man's own best interest, that man's welfare is God's primary concern, and so does righteousness.

This leads us to the biblical understanding of man's love for God and for his neighbor. Jesus summed up man's obligation to God and neighbor in the form of a double commandment: "You shall love the Lord your God with all your heart, and with all your soul, and with all your mind. This is the first and great commandment. And a second is like it. You shall love your neighbor as yourself. On these two commandments depend all the law and the prophets" (Matt. 22:34–40). For a man to love God means that the Christ-event has gripped him so that he behaves as if Christ is at the core of his being. Man's love for God means that because of God's prior activity of love through Christ, he now is willing to become a slave (Luke 27: 7ff.) to Christ, willing to let his movement, existence in the world be determined by his relation to God. "It . . . means regarding God as the ground of one's whole existence, depending upon him without reserve, leaving all care and final responsibility to him, living out of his hand." [33] Like righteousness, it means joining God in his activity on behalf of the oppressed.

This leads us to the second commandment: "Love your neighbor as yourself." To love the neighbor means that we seek to meet his needs. It means being prepared to confront the neighbor as a Thou and doing what is necessary because he is who he is—a creature of God. There is really no need to ask or even discuss the question, "Who is the neighbor?" To accept God's act in Christ at the very core of one's existence means a radical identification with all men. No one is excluded. Every man necessarily becomes one's neighbor; his place in existence becomes ours, including the non-Christian. It is this radical identification with the neighbor which prevents God's grace from becoming "cheap grace" [34] and the mistaking of worship for faith.

To accept God's grace means that because God has acted for all, all men are free—free to respond creatively to that act. It thus becomes the act of Christian love to proclaim the Good News of freedom by actively fighting against all those powers which hold men captive.

With this interpretation in view, we now ask: What does this mean to the black man in America today? What does it mean to speak of God's love to man? Man's response to God? His love of neighbor?

For God to love the black man means that God has made him somebody. The black man does not need to hate himself because he is not white, and he should feel no need to become like others. His blackness, which society despises, is a special creation of God himself. He has worth because God imparts value through loving. It means that God has bestowed on him a new image of himself, so that he can now become what he in fact is. Through God's love, the black man is given the power to *become*, the power to make others recognize him. Because God is "a God of power; of majesty and of might," to love man means that he wills that the black man "reflect in the immediacies of life his power, his majesty and his might." [35]

For the black man to respond to God's love in faith means

that he accepts as truth the new image of himself revealed in Jesus Christ. He now knows that the definition of himself defined by white society is inconsistent with the newly found image disclosed in Christ. In a world which has taught blacks to hate themselves, the new black man does not transcend blackness, but accepts it, loves it as a gift of the Creator. For he knows that until he accepts himself as a being of God in all of its physical blackness, he can love neither God nor neighbor. This may be what one Black Power advocate meant when he said: "Until blacks develop themselves, they can do nothing for humanity." [36] And another who said, "Black Power does not teach hatred; it teaches love. But it teaches us that love, like charity, must begin at home; that it must begin with ourselves, our beautiful black selves." [37]

When St. Paul speaks of being "a new creature" in Christ, the redeemed black man takes that literally. He glorifies blackness, not as a means of glorifying self in the egotistical sense, but merely as an acceptance of the black self as a creature of God.

But what does it mean for the black man to love the neighbor, especially the white neighbor? To love the white man means that the black man *confronts* him as a Thou without any intentions of giving ground by becoming an It. Though the white man is accustomed to addressing an It, in the new black man he meets a Thou. The black man must, if he is not to lose sight of his new-found identity in Christ, be prepared for conflict, for a radical confrontation. As one black man put it: "Profound love can only exist between two equals." [38] The new black man refuses to assume the It-role which whites expect, but addresses them as an equal. This is when the conflict arises.

Therefore the new black man refuses to speak of love without justice and power. Love without the power to guarantee justice in human relations is meaningless. Indeed, there is no place in Christian theology for sentimental love, love without risk or cost. Love demands all, the whole of one's being. Thus, for the black man to believe the Word of God about his love revealed in Christ, he must be prepared to meet head-on the sentimental "Christian" love of whites, which would make him a nonperson.

The insistence that love, power, and justice are inseparable seems to be one of Paul Tillich's contributions to contemporary theology,[39] offsetting the dangerous emphasis on powerlessness or weakness in the face of inhumanity. "Love and Power," writes Tillich, "are often contrasted in such a way that love is identified with a resignation of power and power with a denial of love. Powerless love and loveless power are contrasted. . . . But such an understanding is error and confusion."[40] Therefore he rejects the traditional view, with its emphasis on emotion, as an inadequate representation of love. Since love is "the reunion of the estranged"[41] (and one may be estranged from self as well as from another); and since power is the "possibility of self-affirmation in spite of internal and external negation,"[42] both love and power must be interrelated. Power becomes the possibility of the reunion of self with self and with the other. Without power, love would cease to be love because reunion would be impossible, and being would become nonbeing. That is why Tillich says, "Love is the foundation, not the negation of power."[43] And that is why Black Power is an indispensable element in black-white relations, if we are going to speak from a Christian perspective. Taking his clue from Luther, Tillich speaks to the essence of Black Power and the uniqueness of Christianity when he says, "It is the strange work of love to destroy what is against love."[44] Love conflicts with compulsory power only "when it prevents the aim of love, namely the reunion of the separated."[45]

It seems that whites forget about the necessary interrelatedness of love, justice, and power when they encounter black people. Love becomes emotional and sentimental. This sentimental, condescending love accounts for their desire to "help" by relieving the physical pains of the suffering blacks so they can satisfy their own religious piety and keep the poor powerless. But the new blacks, redeemed in Christ, must refuse their "help" and demand that blacks be confronted as persons. They must say to whites that authentic love is not "help," not giving Christmas baskets but working for political, social, and economic justice, which always means a redistribution of power. It is a kind of power which enables the blacks to fight their own battles and thus keep their dignity. "Powerlessness breeds a race of beggars." [46]

It is evident, then, that the main difficulty which most whites have with Black Power and its relationship to the Christian gospel stems from their own inability to translate traditional theological language into the life situation of black people. The black man's response to God's act in Christ must be different from the white's because his life experiences are different. Christian love is never fully embodied in an act. Love is the motive or the rationale for action. The attempt of some to measure love exclusively by specific actions, such as nonviolence, is theologically incorrect. Christian love comprises the being of a man whereby he behaves as if God is the essence of his existence. It means that God has hold of him and his movement in the world. But this does not take away the finiteness of man, the existential doubt in making decisions in the world. To accept Christ means both self-acceptance and neighbor-acceptance with the existential threat of nonbeing. What existentialists call nonbeing is never removed from man's existence. Thus, the love of self and the love of neighbor, which constitute the heart of one's being in God, never escape the possibility of self-annihilation and destruction of the neighbor. The violence in the cities, which appears to contradict Christian love, is nothing but the black man's attempt to say Yes to his being as defined by God in a world that would make his being into nonbeing. If the riots are the black man's courage to say Yes to himself as a creature of God, and if in affirming self he affirms Yes to the neighbor, then violence may be the black man's expression, sometimes the only possible expression, of Christian love to the white oppressor. From the perspective of a Christian theologian seeking to take seriously the black man's condition in America, what other view is possible?

It seems that the mistake of most whites, religionists included, is their insistence on telling blacks how to respond "as Christians" to racism, insisting that nonviolence is the only appropriate response. But there is an ugly contrast between the sweet, nonviolent language of white Christians and their participation in a violently unjust system. Maybe the oppressor's being is so warped by his own view of himself that every analysis made by him merely reveals his own inflated self-evaluation. Certainly as long as he can count on blacks remaining nonviolent by turning the other cheek and accepting the conditions of slavery, there will be no real pressure to confront the black man as a person. If he can be sure that blacks will not threaten his wealth, his superiority, his power in the world, there will be no need to give up his control of the black man's destiny.

One cannot help but think that most whites "loved" Martin Luther King, Jr., not because of his attempt to free his people, but because his approach was the least threatening to the white power structure. Thus, churchmen and theologians grasped at the opportunity to identify with him so that they could keep blacks powerless and simultaneously appease their own guilt about white oppression. It was only a few years back that King's name was even more radical than that of Rap Brown or Stokely Carmichael. At that time the question was being asked whether civil disobedience was consistent with Christianity. What whites really want is for the black man to respond with that method which best preserves white racism. All this suggests that white judgments about Christian love related to Black Power are as suspect as their other judgments relative to black America.

The Holy Spirit and Black Power

Traditional Christian theology describes the activity of God today in terms of the work of the Holy Spirit. He is the Spirit of God and of Christ at work today in the lives of men accomplishing the work of salvation begun in the election of Israel and continued in Christ. The presence of God and Christ in the manifestation of the outpouring of the Spirit was so evident in the experience of the early Christian community that the Church Fathers thought it theologically necessary to speak of God as Trinity, protecting, on the one hand, the unity of the Godhead and, on the other, the threefold revelation of God as Father, Son, and Holy Spirit.

It is important for our purposes, and for the purposes of traditional theology, to remember that God's manifestation as Spirit is indispensable for a total picture of the Christian God. God was revealed as Spirit in the Old Testament and the New, and his presence today is in the form of Holy Spirit. This, however, should not be taken to mean that God as Spirit in the biblical tradition or contemporary theology is something other than God as Father and Son. In fact, the Holy Spirit is nothing but the Spirit of God and Christ working out his will in the lives of men.

The Holy Spirit is the power of God at work in the world effecting in the life of his people his intended purposes. It is for this reason that Eduard Schweizer says, ". . . the spirit of God is power, power with a moral emphasis." [47] God's Spirit is not just a subjective feeling of piety or inspiration in the hearts of men but, rather, an "active power, that is to say, it is the personal activity of God's will, achieving a moral and religious object." [48] That is why the Bible sometimes identifies the operation of the Spirit with the wind, which manifests power and is at the same time mysterious. "The wind blows where it wills and you hear the sound of it, but you do not know whence it comes nor whither it goes; so it is with every one who is born of the Spirit" (John 3:8).

With the death and resurrection of Christ, the gift of the Spirit to persons—rare in the Old Testament—becomes a possibility for all who respond to God's act in Christ in faithful obedience. The Spirit becomes the power of Christ himself at work in the life of the believer. The mistake of the modern church is to identify the work of God's Spirit in the believer either with private moments of ecstasy or with individual purification from sin, particularly from a short list of ritual pollutants, such as alcohol and tobacco. This is a hopelessly impoverished view. The working of God's Spirit in the life of the believer means an involvement in the world where men are suffering. When the Spirit of God gets hold of a man, he is made a new creature, a creature prepared to move head-on into the evils of this world, ready to die for God. That is why the Holy Spirit is the *power* of God, for it means a continuation of God's work for which Christ died. The work of the Spirit is what happens to a man's total being, a change wherein he is now repelled by suffering and death caused by the bigotry of others. He is repelled because statesmen and politicians say we need more time before black men can have human dignity.

The man possessed by God's Spirit has no time to ask abstract questions about how the poor got to be poor or why blacks are hated by whites. All he knows is that "the Gestapos are busy again, the prisons are filling up, the torturers are once more inventing, perfecting, consulting over their work benches," [49] and he cannot close his eyes to it. Like John Brown who "lived and breathed justice," the man of the Spirit can only say, "Racism is evil, kill it!"

> But we must study the problem . . .
> [Racism] is evil—kill it!
> We will hold a conference . . .
> [Racism] is evil—kill it!
> But our allies . . .
> [Racism] is evil—kill it! [50]

There is no time for talk when men are suffering. For the man of the Spirit, racism is "not a word; it is a fact," a ghetto, poverty, "an event." [51] He, therefore, must join and take sides with the sufferer. To be possessed by God's Spirit means that the believer is willing to be obedient unto death, becoming the means through whom God makes his will known and the vehicle of the activity of God himself.

It should be pointed out here that the work of the Spirit is not always a conscious activity on the part of the persons through whom God works. In fact, God may even use the nonbeliever, as in the case of the Persian emperor Cyrus (Isa. 45). Or he may use persons who are not conscious of being for or against God, but merely against the suffering of men. This seems to be at least part of the point of the parable of the Last Judgment (Matt. 25:31ff.). Men are placed on the right and on the left according to their ministering to the neighbor. Those on the right were surprised: "Lord, when did we see thee hungry and feed thee, or thirsty and give thee drink? And when did we see thee a stranger and welcome thee, or naked and clothe thee? And when did we see thee sick or in prison and visit thee?" (Matt. 25: 37–39). "Their actions were evidently not meant for him, but only for those in trouble." [52] But this is why they are on the right. "Truly, I say to you, as you did it to one of the least of these my brethren you did it to me" (Matt. 25:40). "The cursed, however, who put the same astonished question, are those who want to make their ignorance an excuse for their neglect and thereby prove that they would have been prepared to love their neighbour only if in meeting him they had quite unmistakably met Christ himself." [53] But such men want only to use the neighbor as a means to achieve a private, selfish end. Authentic living according to the Spirit means that one's will becomes God's will, one's actions become God's action. It could be that many will be excluded because their motives were ill-founded. And this may mean that God is not necessarily at work in those places where the Word is truly preached and the sacraments are duly administered (as Reformation theologians defined the Church), but where the naked are clothed, the sick are visited, and the hungry are fed.

Black Power, though not consciously seeking to be Christian, seems to be where men are in trouble. And to the extent that it is genuinely concerned and seeks to meet the needs of the oppressed, it is the work of God's Spirit. By contrast the self-consciously "Christian" person so easily uses the poor as a means to his own salvation. But unless the condition of the poor becomes the condition of the Christian, not because he feels sorry for the poor, but because through the Spirit of Christ he is in fact poor, all acts done on behalf of them are nothing in the eyes of God.

But how can the believer be certain that he is possessed by the Spirit? Or how can he be sure where God is at work? There are no abstract tests or objective guarantees that one is doing the work of God. There is only a subjective certainty in which one knows that he is in touch with the Real, what Paul calls "the Spirit in our hearts, crying 'Abba! Father!' " (Gal. 4:6). It is what Søren Kierkegaard calls "the passion of inwardness." "Faith," writes Kierkegaard, "is the objective uncertainty due to the repulsion of the absurd held fast by the passion of inwardness, which in this instance is intensified to the utmost degree." [54] It is absurd because there are no objective scientific criteria to judge whether one is right. In fact, "He who from the vantage point of a higher knowledge would know his faith as a factor resolved in a higher idea has *eo ipso* ceased to believe." [55] It is an existential certainty which grips the whole of one's being in such a way that now all actions are done in the light of the Ultimate Reality. Karl Barth calls this "the Subjective Reality of Revelation." It is "our freedom to be the children of God and to know and love and praise him in his revelation." [56] There are no rational tests to measure this quality of being grasped in the depths of one's being. The experience is its own evidence, the ultimate datum. To seek for a higher evidence, a more objective proof—such as the Bible, the Fathers, or the Church—implies that such evidence is more real than the encounter itself. According to Hordern, there is nothing the Christian can point to that is more convincing than the relationship itself. The relationship itself carries with it its own power to convince.[57]

Black Power, then, is God's new way of acting in America. It is his way of saying to blacks that they are human beings; he is saying to whites: "Get used to it!"

Whites, as well as some blacks, will find the encounter of Black Power a terrible experience. Like the people of Jesus' day, they will find it hard to believe that God would stoop so low as to reveal himself in and through black people and especially the "undesirable elements." If he has to make himself known through blacks, why not choose the "good Negroes"? But, that is just the point: God encounters men at that level of experience which challenges their being. The real test of whether whites can communicate with blacks as human beings is not what they reply to Ralph Bunche but how they respond to Rap Brown.

III

The White Church and Black Power

Let the Church discover and identify itself with groups of
people that suffer because of unjust situations, and who have
no way of making themselves heard. The Church should be the
voice of those who have no one. The Church must discover
these groups and identify herself with them. Here is the
modern Way of the Cross, the way of Christian responsibility.

Emilio Castro

The meaning of Black Power and its relationship to Christianity
has been the focal point of our discussion thus far. It has been
argued that Black Power is the spirit of Christ himself in the
black-white dialogue which makes possible the emancipation of
blacks from self-hatred and frees whites from their racism.
Through Black Power, blacks are becoming men of worth, and
whites are forced to confront them as human beings.

There is no other spirit in American life so challenging as
the spirit of Black Power. We can see it affecting every major
aspect of American life—economic, political, and social. In major
white and black universities its spirit is manifested in the demand for more emphasis on "black studies." Black students have
literally taken over some administration buildings in an effort
to make white authorities recognize the importance of their demands. In politics, Stokely Carmichael and Charles Hamilton
have given the political implications of Black Power.[1] For them
Black Power in politics means blacks controlling their political

destiny by voting for black people and perhaps eventually forming a coalition with poor whites against middle-class whites. For
some others it means black nationalism. Economically it may
mean boycotting, or building stores for black people. Religiously
or philosophically it means an inner sense of freedom from the
structures of white society which builds its economy on the
labor of poor blacks and whites. It means that the slave now
knows that he is a man, and thus resolves to make the enslaver
recognize him. I contend that such a spirit is not merely compatible with Christianity; in America in the latter twentieth
century it is Christianity.

Some critics of this thesis may ask about the place of the
Church in my analysis. It may appear that its role as an agent
of God in the world has been overlooked. This leads us to an
investigation of the biblical understanding of the Church and
its relationship to white denominational churches.

What Is the Church?

What is the Church and its relationship to Christ and Black
Power? The Church is that people called into being by the
power and love of God to share in his revolutionary activity for
the liberation of man.

Mythically the interrelation of God, man, and the world is
presented in the Genesis picture of the man and the woman in
the garden. Man was created to share in God's creative (revolutionary) activity in the world (Gen. 1:27-28). But through sin
man rejects his proper activity and destiny. He wants to be God,
the creator of his destiny. This is the essence of sin, every man's
desire to become "like God." But in his passion to become super-
human, man becomes subhuman, estranged from the source of
his being, threatening and threatened by his neighbor, trans-
forming a situation destined for intimate human fellowship
into a spider web of conspiracy and violence. God, however, will

not permit man thus to become less than the divine intention for him. He therefore undertakes a course of not-so-gentle persuasion for the liberation and restoration of his creatures.

The call of Abraham was the beginning of this revolutionary activity on behalf of man's liberation from his own sinful pride. This was followed by the exodus, the most significant revelatory act in the Old Testament, which demonstrated God's purposes for man. God showed thereby that he was the Lord of history, that his will for man is not to be thwarted by other human wills. And when Pharaoh said to Moses and Aaron, "The Lord is righteous, and I and my people are wicked" (Exod. 9:27), he was saying that even he recognized the righteousness of God in contrast to the wickedness of men.

The history of Israel is a history of God's election of a special, oppressed people to share in his creative involvement in the world on behalf of man. The call of this people at Sinai into a covenant relationship for a special task may be said to be the beginning of the Church.[2] In the Old Testament, Israel often refers to herself as the *qahal,* the assembly or people of God.[3] Israel is called into being as a people of the covenant in which Yahweh promises to be their God and they his people. Israel's task is to be a partner in God's revolutionary activity and thus to be an example to the whole world of what God intends for all men. By choosing Israel, the oppressed people among the nations, God reveals that his concern is not for the strong but for the weak, not for the enslaver but for the slave, not for whites but for blacks. To express the goal of her striving, Israel spoke of the Day of the Lord and the Kingdom of God, in which God would vindicate his people from oppression and the rule of his righteousness would be recognized by all. This would be the day when the lion would lie down with the lamb and men would beat their swords into plowshares.

In the New Testament, the coming of God in Christ means that the Kingdom of God expected in the Old Testament is now realized in Jesus of Nazareth. The Day of the Lord has come in the life, death, and resurrection of Jesus. This day is no longer future but present in the man Jesus. In him is embodied God's Kingdom in which men are liberated. He is, as Paul says, the "New Adam," who has done for man what man could not do for himself. His death and resurrection mean that the decisive battle has been fought and won, and man no longer has to be a slave to "principalities and powers."

With him also comes a new people which the New Testament calls the *ekklesia* (church). Like the people of Old Israel, they are called into being by God himself—to be his agent in this world until Christ's second coming. Like Old Israel, they are an oppressed people, created to cooperate in God's liberation of all men. Unlike Old Israel, their membership is not limited by ethnic or political boundaries, but includes all who respond in faith to the redemptive act of God in Christ with a willingness to share in God's creative activity in the world. Unlike Old Israel, they do not look forward to the coming of the Kingdom, but know that, in Christ, God's Kingdom has already come and their very existence is a manifestation of it. The Church merely waits for its full consummation in Christ's second coming. Therefore, its sole purpose for being is to be a visible manifestation of God's work in the affairs of men. The Church, then, consists of people who have been seized by the Holy Spirit and who have the determination to live as if all depends on God. It has no will of its own, only God's will; it has no duty of its own, only God's duty. Its existence is grounded in God.

The Church of Christ is not bounded by standards of race, class, or occupation. It is not a building or an institution. It is not determined by bishops, priests, or ministers as these terms are used in their contemporary sense. Rather, the Church is God's suffering people. It is that grouping of men who take seriously the words of Jesus: "Blessed are you when men revile you and persecute you and utter all kinds of evil against you falsely on my account" (Matt. 5:11). The call of God constitutes the Church, and it is a call to suffering. As Bonhoeffer put it:

Man is challenged to participate in the sufferings of God at the hands of a godless world.

He must plunge himself into the life of a godless world, without attempting to gloss over its ungodliness with a veneer of religion or trying to transfigure it. . . . To be a Christian does not mean to be religious in a particular way, to cultivate some particular form of asceticism, . . . but to be a man. It is not some religious act which makes a Christian what he is, but participation in the suffering of God in the life of the world.[4]

"Where Christ is, there is the Church." Christ is to be found, as always, where men are enslaved and trampled under foot; Christ is found suffering with the suffering; Christ is in the ghetto—there also is his Church.

The Church is not defined by those who faithfully attend and participate in the 11:00 A.M. Sunday worship. As Harvey Cox says: "The insistence by the Reformers that the church was 'where the word is rightly preached and the sacraments rightly administered' will simply not do today."[5] It may have been fine for distinguishing orthodoxy from heresy, but it is worthless as a vehicle against modern racism. We must therefore be reminded that Christ was not crucified on an altar between two candles, but on a cross between two thieves. He is not in our peaceful, quiet, comfortable suburban "churches," but in the ghetto fighting the racism of churchly white people.

In the New Testament perspective, the Church has essentially three functions: preaching (*kerygma*), service (*diakonia*), and fellowship (*koinonia*). Preaching means proclaiming to the world what God has done for man in Jesus Christ. The Church tells the world about Christ's victory over alien hostile forces. If we compare Christ's work on the cross with warfare, as Oscar Cullmann[6] and others do, then it is the task of the Church to tell the world that the decisive battle in the war has been fought and won by Christ. Freedom has come! The old tyrants have been displaced, and there is no need for anyone to obey evil powers. The Church, then, is men and women running through the streets announcing that freedom is a reality. This is easily translated into the context of modern racism. God in Christ has set men free from white power, and this means an end to ghettos and all they imply. The Church tells black people to shape up and act like free men because the old powers of white racism are writhing in final agony. The Good News of freedom is proclaimed also to the oppressor, but since he mistakes his enslaving power for life and health he does not easily recognize his own mortal illness or hear the healing word. But the revolution is on, and there is no turning back.

Modern kerygmatic preaching has little to do with white ministers admonishing their people to be nice to "Negroes" or "to obey the law of the land." Nor does it involve inviting a "good Negro" preacher to preach about race relations. Preaching in its truest sense tells the world about Christ's victory and thus invites people to act as if God has won the battle over racism. To preach in America today is to shout "Black Power! Black Freedom."

It is important to remember that the preaching of the Word presents a crisis situation. The hearing of the news of freedom through the preaching of the Word always invites the hearer to take one of two sides: He must either side with the old rulers or the new one. "He that is not for me is against me." There is no neutral position in a war. Even in silence, one is automatically identified as being on the side of the oppressor. There is no place in this war of liberation for nice white people who want to avoid taking sides and remain friends with both the racists and the Negro. To hear the Word is to decide: Are you with us or against us? There is no time for conferences or talk of any sort. If the hearing of the Word and the encounter with the Spirit do not convict you, then talk will be of little avail.

The Church not only preaches the Word of liberation, it joins Christ in his work of liberation. This is *diakonia,* "service." Though the decisive battle has been fought and won over racism, the war is not over. There is still left what G. P. Lewis calls the "mopping-up operations."[7] Just as the war in Europe continued for months after it was "won" at Stalingrad and El Alamein, so the war against the principalities and powers continues after the decisive battle on the cross.[8] We still have to fight racism. The evil forces have been defeated but refuse to admit it. "Although defeated," writes William Hordern, "evil still has sufficient strength to fight a stubborn rear-guard action."[9] It is the task of the Church to join Christ in this fight against evil. Thomas Wieser puts it this way:

The way of the church is related to the fact that the Kyrios Lord himself is on his way in the world, . . . and the church has no choice but to follow him who precedes. Consequently obedience and witness to the Kyrios require the discernment of the opening which he provides and the willingness to step into this opening.[10]

The opening has been made and the Church must follow. To follow means that the Church is more than a talking or a resolution-passing community. Its talk is backed up with relevant involvement in the world as a witness, through action, that what it says is in fact true.

Where is "the opening" that Christ provides? Where does he lead his people? Where indeed, if not in the ghetto. He meets the blacks where they are and becomes one of them. We see him there with his black face and big black hands lounging on a streetcorner. "Oh, but surely Christ is above race." But society is not raceless, any more than when God became a despised Jew. White liberal preference for a raceless Christ serves only to make official and orthodox the centuries-old portrayal of Christ as white. The "raceless" American Christ has a light skin, wavy brown hair, and sometimes—wonder of wonders—blue eyes. For whites to find him with big lips and kinky hair is as offensive as it was for the Pharisees to find him partying with tax-collectors. But whether whites want to hear it or not, *Christ is black, baby,* with all of the features which are so detestable to white society.

To suggest that Christ has taken on a black skin is not theological emotionalism. If the Church is a continuation of the Incarnation, and if the Church and Christ are where the oppressed are, then Christ and his Church must identify totally with the oppressed to the extent that they too suffer for the same reasons persons are enslaved. In America, blacks are oppressed because of their blackness. It would seem, then, that emancipation could only be realized by Christ and his Church becoming black. Thinking of Christ as nonblack in the twentieth century is as theologically impossible as thinking of him as non-Jewish in the first century. God's Word in Christ not only fulfills his purposes for man through his elected people, but also inaugurates a new age in which all oppressed people become his people. In America, that people is a black people. In order to remain faithful to his Word in Christ, his present manifestation must be the very essence of blackness.

It is the job of the Church to become black with him and accept the shame which white society places on blacks. But the Church knows that what is shame to the world is holiness to God. Black is holy, that is, it is a symbol of God's presence in history on behalf of the oppressed man. Where there is black, there is oppression; but blacks can be assured that where there is blackness, there is Christ who has taken on blackness so that what is evil in men's eyes might become good. Therefore Christ is black because he is oppressed, and oppressed because he is black. And if the Church is to join Christ by following his opening, it too must go where suffering is and become black also.

This is what the New Testament means by the service of reconciliation. It is not smoothing things over by ignoring the deep-seated racism in white society. It is freeing the racist of racism by making him confront blacks as men. Reconciliation has nothing to do with the "let's talk about it" attitude, or "it takes time" attitude. It merely says, "Look man, the revolution is on. Whose side are you on?"

The Church is also a fellowship (*koinonia*). This means that the Church must be in its own community what it preaches and what it seeks to accomplish in the world. Through the preaching of the Word, the Church calls the world to be responsible to God's act in Christ, and through its service it seeks to bring it about. But the Church's preaching and service are meaningful only insofar as the Church itself is a manifestation of the preached Word. As Harvey Cox puts it, *koinonia* is "that aspect of the church's responsibility . . . which calls for a visible demonstration of what the church is saying in its kerygma and pointing to in its diakonia."[11] Thus the Church, by definition, contains no trace of racism. Christ "has broken down the dividing walls of hostility" (Eph. 2:14). That is why Karl Barth describes the Church as "God's subjective realization of the atonement."[12]

It is this need to be the sign of the Kingdom in the world which impels the Church continually to ask: "Who in the community does not live according to the spirit of Christ?" This is the kind of question which was so important to the sixteenth-century Anabaptists, and it must be vital for the Church of any age. Speaking to this question, Barth says: "The church which is not deeply disturbed by it is not a Christian church."[13] It cannot be "Christ existing as community" or "Christ's presence in history," as Bonhoeffer would put it, without being seriously concerned about the holiness of its members.

It is true that this concern may cause the community to ask the wrong questions. It may focus on irrelevancies (smoking, dancing, drinking, etc.) rather than on the essential (racism). But it is only through the asking of the question, "What makes men Christians?" that the true Church is able to be Christ in the world. The true Church of Christ must define clearly through its members the meaning of God's act in Christ so that all may know what the Church is up to. There can be no doubt in the minds of its members regarding the nature of its community and its purpose in the world. It must be a community that has accepted Christ's acceptance of us, and in this sense, it must be holy.

At all times and in all situations holy members of the holy church, and therefore Christians, were and are the men assembled in it who are thereto elected by the Lord, called by His Word, and constituted by His Spirit: just so many, no more and no less, these men and no others.[14]

The White Church and Black Power

If the real Church is the people of God, whose primary task is that of being Christ to the world by proclaiming the message of the gospel (*kerygma*), by rendering services of liberation (*diakonia*), and by being itself a manifestation of the nature of the new society (*koinonia*), then the empirical institutionalized white church has failed on all counts. It certainly has not rendered services of reconciliation to the poor. Rather, it illustrates the values of a sick society which oppresses the poor. Some present-day theologians, like Hamilton and Altizer, taking their cue from Nietzsche and the present irrelevancy of the Church to modern man, have announced the death of God. It seems, however, that their chief mistake lies in their apparent identification of God's reality with the signed-up Christians. If we were to identify the work of God with the white church, then, like Altizer, we must "will the death of God with a passion of faith." Or as Camus would say, "If God *did* exist, we should have to abolish him."

The white church has not merely failed to render services to the poor, but has failed miserably in being a visible manifestation to the world of God's intention for humanity and in proclaiming the gospel to the world. It seems that the white church is not God's redemptive agent but, rather, an agent of the old society. It fails to create an atmosphere of radical obedience to Christ. Most church fellowships are more concerned about drinking or new buildings or Sunday closing than about children who die of rat bites or men who are killed because they want to be treated like men. The society is falling apart for want of moral leadership and moral example, but the white church passes innocuously pious resolutions and waits to be congratulated.

It is a sad fact that the white church's involvement in slavery and racism in America simply cannot be overstated. It not only failed to preach the kerygmatic Word but maliciously contributed to the doctrine of white supremacy. Even today all of the Church's institutions—including its colleges and universities —reveal its white racist character. Racism has been a part of the life of the Church so long that it is virtually impossible for even the "good" members to recognize the bigotry perpetuated by the Church. Its morals are so immoral that even its most sensitive minds are unable to detect the inhumanity of the Church on the black people of America. This is at least one of the suggestions by Kyle Haselden, who was in most cases a very perceptive white southern churchman:

We must ask whether our morality is itself immoral, whether our codes of righteousness are, when applied to the Negro, a violation and distortion of the Christian ethic. Do we not judge what is right and what is wrong in racial relationships by a righteousness which is itself unrighteous, by codes and creeds which are themselves immoral? [15]

The question is asked and the answer is obvious to the astute observer. The Church has been guilty of the gravest sin of all—"the enshrining of that which is immoral as the highest morality." [16] Jesus called this the sin against the Holy Spirit. It is unforgivable because it is never recognized.

Pierre Berton puts it mildly:

In . . . the racial struggle, there is revealed the same pattern of tardiness, apathy, non-commitment, and outright opposition by the church. . . . Indeed, the history of the race struggle in the United States has been to a considerable extent the history of the Protestant rapport with the status quo. From the beginning, it was the church that put its blessing on slavery and sanctioned a caste system that continues to this day.[17]

As much as white churchmen may want to hedge on this issue, it is not possible. The issue is clear: Racism is a complete denial of the Incarnation and thus of Christianity. Therefore, the white denominational churches are unchristian. They are a manifestation of both a willingness to tolerate it and a desire to perpetuate it.

The old philosophical distinction between the primary and secondary qualities of objects provides an analogy here, where only the primary qualities pertain to the essence of the thing. Regarding the Church, are not fellowship and service primary qualities, without which the "church" is not the Church? Can we still speak of a community as being Christian if that body is racist through and through? It is my contention that the racism implies the absence of fellowship and service, which are primary qualities, indispensable marks of the Church. To be racist is to fall outside the definition of the Church. In our time, the issue of racism is analogous to the Arian Controversy of the fourth century. Athanasius perceived quite clearly that if Arius' views were tolerated, Christianity would be lost. But few white churchmen have questioned whether racism was a similar denial of Jesus Christ. Even Haselden, certainly one of the most sensitive of the white churchmen who have written on the subject, can speak of white Christian racists.

If there is any contemporary meaning of the Antichrist (or "the principalities and powers"), the white church seems to be a manifestation of it. It is the enemy of Christ. It was the white "Christian" church which took the lead in establishing slavery as an institution and segregation as a pattern in society by sanctioning all-white congregations. As Frank Loescher pointed out, its very existence as an institution is a symbol of the "philosophy of white supremacy." [18] "Long before the little signs—'White Only' and 'Colored'—appeared in the public utilities they had appeared in the church." [19] Haselden shows clearly the work of the Church in setting the pattern which later became general law for all of America:

First came the segregation of the Negro within the church; then followed the separation of the churches by the "spontaneous" withdrawal of the Negro Christians; much later, the elaborate patterns of segregation were to arise in the church and in secular society.[20]

With its all-white congregations, it makes racism a respectable attitude. By remaining silent it creates an ethos which dehumanizes blacks. It is the Church which preaches that blacks are inferior to whites—if not by *word,* certainly by "moral" example.

In the old slavery days, the Church preached that slavery was a divine decree, and it used the Bible as the basis of its authority.

Not only did Christianity fail to offer the Negro hope of freedom in this world, but the manner in which Christianity was communicated to him tended to degrade him. The Negro was taught that his enslavement was due to the fact that he had been cursed by God. His very color was a sign of the curse which he had received as a descendant of Ham. Parts of the Bible were carefully selected to prove that God had intended that the Negro should be the servant of the white man and that he would always be a "hewer of wood and a drawer of water." [21]

Several ministers even wrote books justifying slavery. "It may be," wrote George D. Armstrong in *The Christian Doctrine of Slavery,* "that *Christian slavery* is God's solution of the problem [relation of labor and capital] about which the wisest statesmen of Europe confess themselves at fault." [22] In another book, *Slavery Ordained of God,* Fred A. Ross wrote that "slavery is ordained of God, . . . to continue for the good of the slave, the good of the master, the good of the whole American family, until another and better destiny may be unfolded." [23]

Today that same Church sets the tone for the present inhumanity to blacks by remaining silent as blacks are killed for wanting to be treated like human beings. Like other segments of this society, the Church emphasizes obedience to the law of the land without asking whether the law is racist in character or without even questioning the everyday deadly violence which laws and law enforcers inflict on blacks in the ghetto. They are quick to condemn Black Power as a concept and the violence in the ghetto without saying a word about white power and its 350 years of constant violence against blacks. It was the Church which placed God's approval on slavery and today places his blessings on the racist structure of American society. As long as whites can be sure that God is on their side, there is potentially no limit to their violence against anyone who threatens the American racist way of life. Genocide is the logical conclusion of racism. It happened to the American Indian, and there is ample reason to believe that America is prepared to do the same to blacks.

Many writers have shown the Church's vested interest in slavery and racism in America.[24] At first the "white Christian" questioned the Christianizing of the slave because of the implications of equality in the Bible and because of the fear that education might cause the slave to fight for his freedom. Slave masters at first forbade the baptism of slaves on the ground that it was an invasion of their property rights. But the churchmen assured them that there was no relationship between Christianity and freedom in civil matters. In the words of the Bishop of London:

Christianity, and the embracing of the Gospel, does not make the least Alteration in Civil property, or in any of the Duties which belong to Civil Relations; but in all these Respects, it continues Persons just in the same State as it found them. The Freedom which Christianity gives, is a Freedom from the Bondage of Sin and Satan, and from the Dominion of Men's Lust and Passions and inordinate Desires; but as to their outward Condition, whatever that was before, whether bond or free, their being baptized and becoming Christians, makes no matter of Change in it.[25]

In fact some churchmen argued that Christianity made blacks better slaves. When slaves began to get rebellious about their freedom, according to a Methodist missionary, "it was missionary influence that moderated their passions, kept them in the steady course of duty, and prevented them from sinning against God by offending against the laws of man. Whatever outbreaks or insurrections at any time occurred, no Methodist slave was ever proved guilty of incendiarism or rebellion for more than seventy years, namely from 1760 to 1833." [26]

Many ministers even owned slaves. In 1844, 200 Methodist traveling preachers owned 1,600 slaves, and 1,000 local preachers owned 10,000 slaves. This fact alone indicates the white Methodist Church's tolerance and propagation of the slave system. There is no evidence that it saw any real contradiction between slavery and essential Christianity.

Some northern white Methodist churchmen would probably remind me that the Church split precisely over that issue in 1844. This seems to suggest that at least the north was against slavery. If the north was against slavery, it nevertheless had no intention of viewing blacks as men. Northern churchmen are reminded that it was in their section of the country that "free Negroes" seceded from various white churches because of intolerable humiliation by whites. It was northerners who pulled Richard Allen and his companions from their knees as they knelt at prayer at St. George's Methodist Episcopal Church in Philadelphia. "We all went out of the church in a body," wrote Allen, "and they were no more plagued with us in the church." [27] There is no evidence at all that the north was more humane than the south in its treatment of blacks in the churches. The north could appear to be more concerned about the blacks because of their work toward the abolition of slavery. But the reason is clear: Slavery was not as vital to their economy as it was to the south's.

Some southern churchmen might argue that the Church in the pre-Civil War days was indeed a real expression of their concern for blacks. It was an integrated Church! Surprisingly, H. Richard Niebuhr suggests that the worship of white and black people together was an indication that the great revival and the democratic doctrines of the Revolution which fostered the sense of equality had "pricked the conscience of the churches on the subject of slavery." [28]

White and black worshipped together and, at their best, sought to realize the brotherhood Jesus had practiced and Paul had preached. There were many significant exceptions, it is true. But the general rule was that the two races should be united in religion. . . . In the Methodist and Baptist churches, . . . it was the conviction of the essential equality of all souls before God which inspired the white missionary and an occasional master to share the benefits of the common gospel in a common church with members of the other race.[29]

Apparently, Niebuhr's identity with the oppressor got the best of his theological and sociological analysis. For it is clear that "integration" was a practice in the southern churches because, as Niebuhr himself says, it was "the less of two evils." It was dangerous to the slave system to allow slaves to have independent uncontrolled churches. The abolitionist activity in the northern black churches and the Nat Turner revolt of 1831 reaffirmed this fear. Laws were even passed which prevented the education of blacks and the assembly of more than five blacks without white supervision. Rather than being a demonstration of brotherhood or equality, the "integration" in the churches was a means of keeping a close watch on blacks. Haselden is right about the Church. It was and is the "mother of racial patterns," the "purveyor of arrant sedatives," and the "teacher of immoral moralities."

The Quakers were the only denominational group which showed any signs of radical obedience to Christ. Its leaders, George Fox and George Keith, declared clearly the contradiction between slavery and the gospel of Christ. An example of the Quaker view of slavery is illustrated by the resolution of 1688, passed in Germantown:

Now tho' they are black, we cannot conceive there is more liberty to have them slaves, as it is to have other white ones. There is a saying, that we shall doe to all men, like as we will be done our selves: macking no difference of what generation, descent, or Colour they are. And those who steal or robb men, and those who buy or purchase them, are they not all alicke? Here is liberty of Conscience, wch is right and reasonable, here ought to be lickewise liberty of the body, except of evildoers, wch is an other case. But to bring men hither, or to robb and sell them against their will, we stand against.[30]

It is unfortunate that such men were in the minority even among the Quakers. There was the temptation to let economics, rather than religion, determine one's actions. The Quakers, like most groups who could afford it, owned slaves. But the spirit of freedom and liberty in civil matters was at least the concern of some Quakers, which is more than can be said of others.

In light of this history it is not surprising that the white churchmen have either condemned Black Power, or, as is more often the case, joined the other silent intellectuals in our colleges and universities. They have never championed black freedom. During the most fervent period of lynching,[31] the Church scarcely said a word against it. Loetscher's study of the twenty-five major denominations comprising the Federal Council of Churches of Christ in America shows that until 1929 most churches scarcely uttered a word about white inhumanity toward blacks. In fact, Gunnar Myrdal pointed out, "Methodist and Baptist preachers were active in reviving the Ku Klux Klan after the First World War." [32] There is little question that the Church has been and is a racist institution, and there is little sign that she even cares about it.

So far as the major denominations are concerned, it is the story of indifference, vacillation, and duplicity. . . . It is a history in which the church not only compromised its ethic to the mood and practice of the times but was itself actively unethical, sanctioning the enslavement of human beings, producing the patterns of segregation, urging upon the oppressed Negro the extracted sedatives of the Gospel, and promulgating a doctrine of interracial morality which is itself immoral.[33]

Some churchmen probably would want to point out their "unselfish involvement" in the civil rights struggle of the 1950's and 1960's. It was a black man, Martin Luther King, Jr., who challenged the conscience of this nation by his unselfish giving of his time and eventually his life for the poor blacks and whites of America. During the initial stages of his civil-dis-obedience campaign, most white churchmen stood silently by and criticized with their political cohorts. And most who eventually joined him in his work were "Johnnies-come-lately." Even here their participation reminds one of the white churchmen of the pre-Civil War era. As long as the south was the target, northern churchmen could assure themselves that it was a southern problem, totally unrelated to their own northern parishes. Most thus came to think of themselves as missionaries for Christ in a foreign land. But when King brought his work north, many retreated and complained that he was confusing politics with religion. King only regained his popularity among northern churchmen after the emergence of the concept of Black Power. They came to view King's nonviolence as the less of two evils. I am convinced that King's death was due to an ethos created by the white church, which permits whites to kill blacks at will without any fear of reprisal. Few white men have been convicted and imprisoned for slaying a black or a white involved in civil rights.

Since the emergence of the recent rebellion in the cities, it seems that the most the white churches do is to tell blacks to obey the law of the land. Occasionally, a church body passes a harmless resolution. Imagine, men dying of hunger, children maimed from rat bites, women dying of despair—and the Church passes a resolution. Perhaps it is impossible to prevent riots, but one can fight against the conditions which cause them. The white church is placed in question because of its contribution to a structure which produces riots. Some churchmen may reply: "We do condemn the deplorable conditions which produce urban riots. We do condemn racism and all the evils arising from it." But to the extent that this is true, the Church, with the exception of a few isolated individuals, voices its condemnation in the style of resolutions that are usually equivocal and almost totally unproductive. If the condemnation was voiced, it was not understood! The Church should speak in a style which avoids abstractions. Its language must be backed up with relevant involvement in the affairs of people who suffer. It must be a grouping whose community life and personal involvement are coherent with its language about the gospel.

The Church does not appear to be a community willing to pay up personally. It is not a community which views every command of Jesus as a call to the cross. It appears, instead, as an institution whose existence depends on the evils which produce the riots in the cities. With this in mind, we must say that when a minister condemns the rioters and blesses by silence the conditions which produce the riots, he gives up his credentials as a Christian minister and becomes inhuman. He is an animal, just like those who, backed by an ideology of racism, order the structure of this society on the basis of white supremacy. We need men who refuse to be animals and are resolved to pay the price, so that all men can be something more than animals.

Whether Black Power advocates are that grouping, we will have to wait and see. But the Church has shown many times that it loves life and is not prepared to die for others. It has not really gone where the action is with a willingness to die for the neighbor, but has remained aloof from the sufferings of men. It is a chaplaincy to sick middle-class egos. It stands (or sits) condemned by its very whiteness.

This leads one to conclude that Christ is operating outside the denominational white church. The real Church of Christ is that grouping which identifies with the suffering of the poor by becoming one with them. While we should be careful in drawing the line, the line must nevertheless be drawn. The Church includes not only the Black Power community but all men who view their humanity as inextricably related to every man. It is that grouping with a demonstrated willingness to die for the prevention of the torture of others, saying with Bonhoeffer, "When Christ calls a man, he bids him come and die."

Is there any hope for the white church? Hope is dependent upon whether it will ask from the depths of its being with God: "What must I do to be saved?" The person who seriously asks that question is a person capable of receiving God's forgiveness. It is time for the white church to ask that question with a willingness to do all for Christ. Like the Philippian jailers who put the question to St. Paul, the answer is the same for the white church as it was to them: *Repent,* and believe on the Lord and Saviour Jesus Christ! There is no other way. It must own that it has been and is a racist institution whose primary purpose is the perpetuation of white supremacy. But it is not enough to be sorry or to admit wrong. To repent involves change in one's whole being. In the Christian perspective, it means conversion.

Speaking of Jesus' understanding of repentance, Bornkamm says: It means "to lay hold on the salvation which is already at hand, and to give up everything for it." [34] This involves a willingness to renounce self and the world and to grasp the gift of salvation now here in Jesus Christ. But there is no repentance without obedience and there is no obedience without action. And this is always action in the world with Christ fighting the evils which hold men captive.

For the white churches this means a radical reorientation of their style in the world toward blacks. It means that they must change sides, giving up all claims to lofty neutrality. It means that they will identify utterly with the oppressed, thus inevitably tasting the sting of oppression themselves. It means that they will no longer "stand silently or march weakly protesting" but will join the advocates of Black Power in their unambiguous identification "with the oppressed and with the revolutions made by the oppressed." [35] A racist pattern has been set, and the Church has been a contributor to the pattern. Now it must break that pattern by placing its life at stake.

Black Power and American Theology

In a culture which rewards "patriots" and punishes "dissenters," it is difficult to be prophetic and easy to perform one's duties in the light of the objectives of the nation as a whole. This was true for the state church of Germany during the Third Reich, and it is true now of the white church in America as blacks begin to question seriously their place in this society. It is always much easier to point to the good amid the evil as a means of rationalizing one's failure to call into question the evil itself. It is easier to identify with the oppressor as he throws sops to the poor than to align oneself with the problems of the poor as he endures oppression. Moreover, the moral and religious implications of any act of risk are always sufficiently cloudy to make it impossible to be certain of right action. Because man is finite, he can never reach that state of security in which he is free of anxiety when he makes moral decisions. This allows the irresponsible religious man to grasp a false kind of religious and political security by equating law and order with Christian morality. If someone calls his attention to the inhumanity of the political system toward others, he can always explain his loyalty to the state by suggesting that this system is the least evil of any other existing political state. He can also point to the lack of clarity regarding the issues, whether they concern race relations or the war in Vietnam. This will enable him to compartmentalize the various segments of the societal powers so that he can rely on other disciplines to give the word on the appropriate course of action. This seems to characterize the style of many religious thinkers as they respond to the race problem in America.

Therefore, it is not surprising that the sickness of the Church in America is also found in the main stream of American religious thought. As with the Church as a whole, theology remains conspicuously silent regarding the place of the black man in American society. In the history of modern American theology, there are few dissenters on black slavery and the current black oppression among the teachers and writers of theology. And those who do speak are usually unclear. Too often their comments are but a replica of the current cultural ethos, drawing frequently from nontheological disciplines for the right word on race relations.

More often, however, theologians simply ignore the problem of color in America. Any theologian involved in professional societies can observe that few have attempted to deal seriously with the problem of racism in America. It is much easier to deal with the textual problems associated with some biblical book or to deal "objectively" with a religious phenomenon than it is to ask about the task of theology in the current disintegration of society. It would seem that it is time for theology to make a radical break with its identity with the world by seeking to bring to the problem of color the revolutionary implications of the gospel of Christ. It is time for theology to leave its ivory tower and join the real issues, which deal with dehumanization of blacks in America. It is time for theologians to relate their work to life-and-death issues, and in so doing to execute its function of bringing the Church to a recognition of its task in the world.

For the sickness of the Church in America is intimately involved with the bankruptcy of American theology. When the Church fails to live up to its appointed mission, it means that theology is partly responsible. Therefore, it is impossible to criticize the Church and its lack of relevancy without criticizing theology for its failure to perform its function.

Theology functions within the Church. Its task is to make sure that the "church" is the Church. The mission of the Church is to announce and to act out the gospel it has received. When the Church fails in its appointed task by seeking to glorify itself rather than Jesus Christ, it is the job of theology to remind her what the true Church is, for theology is that discipline which has the responsibility of continually examining the proclamation of the Church in the light of Jesus Christ. "Dogmatic theology is the scientific test to which the Christian church puts herself regarding the language about God which is peculiar to her." [36] The task of theology, then, is to criticize and revise the language of the Church. This includes not only language as uttered speech but the language of radical involvement in the world. The Church not only speaks of God in "worship" but as it encounters the world with the gospel of Jesus Christ. It is the task of theology to make sure that the Church's thoroughly human speech, whether word or deed, agrees with the essence of the Church, that is, with Jesus Christ who is "God in his gracious approach to man in revelation and reconciliation." [37]

The Church cannot remain aloof from the world because Christ is in the world. Theology, then, if it is to serve the need of the Church must become "worldly theology." This means that it must make sure that the Church is in the world and that its word and deed are harmonious with Jesus Christ. It must make sure that the Church's language about God is relevant to every new generation and its problems. It is for this reason that the definitive theological treatise can never be written. Every generation has its own problems, as does every nation. Theology is not, then, an intellectual exercise but a worldly risk.

American theology has failed to take that worldly risk. It has largely ignored its domestic problems on race. It has not called the Church to be involved in confronting this society with the meaning of the Kingdom in the light of Christ. Even though it says, with Tillich, that theology "is supposed to satisfy two basic needs: the statement of the truth of the Christian message and the interpretation of this truth for every new generation," [38] it has virtually ignored the task of relating the truth of the gospel to the problem of race in America. The lack of a relevant, risky theological statement suggests that theologians, like others, are unable to free themselves from the structures of this society.

The close identity of American theology with the structures of society may also account for the failure to produce theologians comparable in stature to Europeans like Bultmann, Barth, and Bonhoeffer. Some try to account for this by pointing to the youth of America; but that seems an insufficient explanation, since other disciplines appear to hold their own. The real reasons are immensely complex. But one cogent explanation is that most American theologians are too closely tied to the American structure to respond creatively to the life situation of the Church in this society. Instead of seeking to respond to the problems which are unique to this country, most Americans look to Europe for the newest word worth theologizing about. Most graduate students in theology feel that they must go to Germany or somewhere else in Europe because that is where things are happening in the area of theology. Little wonder that American theology is predominantly "footnotes on the Germans." Theology here is largely an intellectual game unrelated to the issues of life and death. It is impossible to respond creatively and prophetically to the life-situational problems of society without identifying with the problems of the disinherited and unwanted in society. Few American theologians have made that identification with the poor blacks in America but have themselves contributed to the system which enslaves black people. The seminaries in America are probably the most obvious sign of the irrelevance of theology to life. Their initiative in responding to the crisis of black people in America is virtually unnoticeable. Their curriculum generally is designed for young white men and women who are preparing to serve all-white churches. Only recently have seminaries sought to respond to the black revolution by reorganizing their curriculum to include courses in "black studies" and inner-city involvements; and this is due almost exclusively to the insistence of black students. Most seminaries still have no courses in black church history and their faculties and administrators are largely white. This alone gives support to the racist assumption that blacks are unimportant.

In Europe the situation seems to be somewhat different. Karl Barth's theology was born in response to the political and economic crisis of Germany. He began his career as a liberal theologian; he believed that the Kingdom of God would soon be achieved through the establishment of a socialist society. He put his confidence in the latent resources of humanity; and this meant that Barth, along with many liberal theologians of his day, believed in the adequacy of the religious man, the adequacy of religion, and the security of the culture and civilization. The First World War shattered his hope of the Kingdom of God on earth. The "civilized man" who was supposed to be moving steadily, even rapidly, toward perfection had cast himself into an orgy of destruction. In the wake of the war came Communism and Fascism, both of which denied Christian values. As a result of the war and its aftermath, Barth felt that the problem of man was much more desperate than most people realized and would not be solved simply by changing the economic structure. For a while Barth was in a state of shock. In particular he was burdened with the task of declaring the Christian message to his congregation every Sunday. What could he say? People did not want to hear, he was quite sure, his own man-made philosophy or his own opinions.

In due time Barth was led from his anthropocentric conception of Christianity to a thoroughgoing theocentric conception. He was led from trust in man to complete trust in God alone. He was convinced that he could not identify God's Word with man's word. No human righteousness can be equated with divine righteousness; no human act can be synonymous with God's act. Even the so-called good which man does in this world counts as nothing in God's eyes. To identify God's righteousness with human righteousness is to fail to see the "infinite qualitative distinction" between God and man, the distinction between that which is human and that which is divine.

This radical change in Barth's theological perspective had nothing to do with abstract theological thinking but with his confrontation with the political, economic, and social situation of Germany. It was the rise of a new political order that caused Barth to launch a devastating and relentless attack on natural theology. When American theologians picked up the problem, they apparently did so without really knowing that for Barth and his sympathizers the natural theology issue was not merely an intellectual debate but an event, an event about the life and death of men. Observing the rise of Hitler during the 1930's, Barth saw clearly the danger of identifying man's word with God's Word. To say that God's Word is wholly unlike man's word means that God stands in judgment against all political systems. The work of the state can never be identified or confused with God's Word. In Hitler's campaign against the Jews, an alien god dominated Germany; men were being slaughtered on his altar. It was no time for caution or lofty "objectivity." When Barth said "Nein!"—no natural theology, no blending of the Word of God and the word of man—the *political* implication was clear: Hitler is the Antichrist; God has set his face against the Third Reich.

Americans have generally agreed that Barth's rejection of natural theology was a mistake. Is that because American theologians still see a close relationship between the structures of this society and Christianity? As long as there is no absolute difference between God and man, it is possible to view America as the "land of the free and the home of the brave," despite the oppression of blacks. As long as theology is identified with the system, it is impossible to criticize it by bringing the judgment of God's righteousness upon it.

Barth's theology may serve as an example of how to relate theology to life. The whole of his theology represents a constant attempt to engage the Church in life situations. Its notable development (compare *Romans* with *The Humanity of God*) is clearly a response to the new problems which men face in worldly involvement.

If American theology is going to serve the needs of the Church by relating the gospel to the political, economic, and social situation of America, it must cut its adoring dependence upon Europe as the place to tell us what theology ought to be talking about. Some European theologians, like Barth and Bonhoeffer, may serve as examples of how to relate theology to life, but not in defining *our* major issues.

There is a need for a theology of revolution, a theology which radically encounters the problems of the disinherited black people in America in particular and the oppressed people of color throughout the world in general. As Joseph Washington puts it:

> In the twentieth century white Protestantism has concentrated its personnel, time, energy, and finances on issues that it has deemed more significant than the "American Dilemma": pacifism, politics, liberal versus conservative controversies, prohibition, socialism, Marxism, labor and management aspects of economic justice, civil liberties, totalitarianism, overseas mission, fascism, war and peace, reorganization of ecclesiastical structures, and ecumenical issues.[39]

It has overlooked the unique problem of the powerless blacks.

In this new era of Black Power, the era in which blacks are sick of white power and are prepared to do anything and give everything for freedom now, theology cannot afford to be silent. Not to speak, not to "do theology" around this critical problem, is to say that the black predicament is not crucial to Christian faith. At a moment when blacks are determined to stand up as human beings even if they are shot down, the Word of the cross certainly is focused upon them. Will no one speak that Word to the dead and dying? Theologians confronted by this question may distinguish three possible responses. Some will, timidly or passionately, continue to appeal (mistakenly) to Paul's dictum about the "powers that be." We will have law-and-order theologians as we have law-and-order pastors and laymen. Others will insist that theology as such is necessarily unrelated to social upheaval. These men will continue as in a vacuum, writing footnotes on the Aramaic substratum of Mark's Gospel or on the authorship of the *Theologia Germanica* or on the "phenomenon" of faith. Could a black man hope that there are still others who, *as theologians,* will join the oppressed in their fight for freedom? These theologians will speak unequivocally of revelation, Scripture, God, Christ, grace, faith, Church, ministry, and hope, so that the message comes through loud and clear: *The black revolution is the work of Christ.*

If theology fails to re-evaluate its task in the light of Black Power, the emphasis on the death of God will not add the needed dimension. This will mean that the white church and white theology are dead, not God. It will mean that God will choose another means of implementing his word of righteousness in the world. It will mean also that the burden of the gospel is placed solely on the shoulders of the oppressed, without any clear word from the "church." This leads us to our last concern, the black church. It is indeed possible that the only redemptive forces left in the denominational churches are to be found in the segregated black churches.

The white response so far, in and out of the Church, is, "Not yet," which in the twisted rhetoric of the land of the free means, "Never!" "Law and order" is the sacred incantation of the priests of the old order; and the faithful respond with votes, higher police budgets, and Gestapo legislation. Private and public arsenals of incredible destructive force testify to the determination of a sick and brutal people to put an end to black revolution and indeed to black people. The black man has violated the conditions under which he is permitted to breathe, and the air is heavy with the potential for genocide. The confrontation of black people as real persons is so strange and out of harmony with the normal pattern of white behavior that most whites cannot even begin to understand the meaning of black humanity.

In this situation of revolution and reaction, the Church must decide where its identity lies. Will it continue its chaplaincy to the forces of oppression, or will it embrace the cause of liberation, proclaiming in word and deed the gospel of Christ?

IV

The Black Church and Black Power

> The progress of emancipation . . . is . . . certain: It
> is certain because that God who has made of one blood all
> nations of men, and who is said to be no respector of
> persons, has so decreed. . . . Did I believe that it would
> always continue, and that man to the end of time would be
> permitted with impunity to usurp the same undue authority
> over his fellows, I would . . . ridicule the religion of
> the Saviour of the world. . . . I would consider my bible
> as a book of false and delusive fables, and commit it to
> flame; Nay, I would still go further: I would at once
> confess myself an atheist, and deny the existence of a holy
> God.
>
> *The Rev. Nathaniel Paul, July 5, 1827*

The black church was born in slavery. Its existence symbolizes a people who were completely stripped of their African heritage as they were enslaved by the "Christian" white man. The white master forbade the slave from any remembrance of his homeland. The mobility created by the slave trade, the destruction of the family, and the prohibition of African languages served to destroy the social cohesion of the African slaves. The slave was a *no-thing* in the eyes of the master, who did everything possible to instill this sense of nothingness in the mentality of the slave. The slave was rewarded and punished according to his adherence to the view of himself defined exclusively by the master.

The black man was shackled in a hostile white world without any power to make the white man recognize him as a person. He had to devise means of survival. This accounts for the slave's preoccupation with death. Death was a compelling and ever-present reality for the slave "because of the cheapness with which his life was regarded. The slave was a tool, a thing, a utility, a commodity, but he was not a person. He was faced constantly with the imminent threat of death, of which the terrible overseer was the symbol; and the awareness that he (the slave) was only chattel property, and dramatization." [1]

> Death is gwinter lay his cold icy hands on me, Lord.
> Death is gwinter lay his cold icy hands on me, Lord.
> One mornin' I was walkin' alone
> I heard a voice and I saw no man
> Said go in peace and sin no more,
> Yo' sins fo'given an' yo' soul set free.
> One of dese mornin's it won't be long,
> Yo'll look fo' me an' I'll be gone.

The black church was the creation of a black people whose daily existence was an encounter with the overwhelming and brutalizing reality of white power. For the slaves it was the sole source of personal identity and the sense of community. Though slaves had no social, economic, or political ties as a people, they had one humiliating factor in common—serfdom! The whole of their being was engulfed in a system intent on their annihilation as persons. Their responses to this overwhelming fact of their existence ranged from suicide to outright rebellion. But few slaves committed suicide. Most refused to accept the white master's definition of black humanity and rebelled with every ounce of humanity in them. The black church became the home base for revolution. Some slaves even rebelled to the point of taking up arms against the white world. Others used the church as a means of transporting the slaves to less hostile territory. Northern independent black churches were " 'stations' in the 'underground railroad'; at which an escaping slave could get means

either to become established in the North or to go to Canada." [2]
Most used the church as a platform for announcing *freedom*
and *equality*.

The black churchman did not accept white interpretations of
Christianity, which suggested the gospel was concerned with
freedom of the soul and not the body. While it is true that most
of the Spirituals are otherworldly and compensatory in character
and that many black preachers pointed to a "land flowing with
milk and honey," this fact must be viewed in the light of the
ever-present dehumanizing reality of white power. It is because
whites completely destroyed their hopes in this world that blacks
sang "I's So Glad Trouble Don't Last Always" and "I Know
de Udder Worl' Is Not Like Dis." A large majority of black
slaves refused to believe that God was irrelevant, but, as they
looked at this life, he appeared not to care. Therefore, in order
to cling to hope, the average black slave had to look forward
to another reality beyond time and space.

It should be emphasized, however, that even the slaves who
looked forward to a new life in heaven did not accept the view
of the white preacher that God ordained slavery for them. White
power may have persuaded some to be passive and accept the
present reality of serfdom; but generally when slaves sang of
heaven, it was because they realized the futility of rebellion and
not because they accepted slavery.

Sometimes it is forgotten that not all of the Spirituals are
otherworldly and compensatory. Some are protesting and rebellious in character. Comparing their own enslavement with
Israelite bondage in Egypt, they sang "Go Down, Moses." The
approach may be subtle, but it is clear:

> When Israel was in Egypt's land,
> Let my people go:
> Oppressed so hard they could not stand,
> Let my people go:
> Go down, Moses, 'way down in Egypt's land;
> Tell old pharaoh—Let my people go.

Even more militant was "Oh, Freedom!" The black slave knew that to fight for freedom is to do the work of God. For him death was preferable to life if the latter must be in slavery. Consequently, he sang: "Oh, freedom! Oh freedom! Oh freedom o-ver me! an' be-fo' I'd be a slave, I'd be buried in my grave, and go home to my Lord an' be free."

Other Spirituals which revealed the slave's determination to relate Christianity to a life of freedom in this world are: "I'm Going to Lay Down My Life for My Lord," "Lord, I Want to Be a Christian in My Heart," "I'm A-going to Do All I Can for My Lord," and "I Want to Live so God Can Use Me." There is no suggestion here that Christianity is merely private, isolated, and unrelated to the conditions of this life. Christianity has to do with fighting with God against the evils of this life. One does not sit and wait on God to do all the fighting, but joins him in the fight against slavery. Therefore, they sang, comparing themselves with Joshua, "Joshua Fit de Battle of Jericho."

The Black Church before the Civil War

The birth of the independent black churches and the teaching of the free black preachers show clearly that Christianity and earthly freedom were inseparable for the black man. The black church was born in protest. In this sense, it is the precursor of Black Power. Unlike the white church, its reality stemmed from the eschatological recognition that freedom and equality are at the essence of humanity, and thus segregation and slavery are diametrically opposed to Christianity. Freedom and equality made up the central theme of the black church; and protest and action were the early marks of its uniqueness, as the black man fought for freedom. White missionaries sought to extol the virtues of the next world, but blacks were more concerned about their freedom in this world. Ironically it was the black man's deep concern for freedom and equality which led him to accept Christianity. He saw that the white master's religion was the best way to freedom.

There are independent black churches today because black people refuse to accept the white master's view of the Christian faith. As early as 1787 Richard Allen and his followers walked out of St. George's Methodist Episcopal Church at Philadelphia because they refused to obey the dictates of white superiority. Allen describes the experiences in this manner:

We had not been long upon our knees before I heard considerable scuffling and low talking. I raised my head up and saw one of the trustees, H—— M——, having hold of the Reverend Absalom Jones, pulling him up off his knees, and saying, "You must get up—you must not kneel here." Mr. Jones replied, "Wait until prayer is over." Mr. H—— M—— said, "No, you must get up now, or I will call for aid and force you away." Mr. Jones said, "Wait until prayer is over, and I will trouble you no more." With that he beckoned to one of the other trustees, Mr. L—— S—— to come to his assistance. He came, and went to William White to pull him up. By this time prayer was over, and we all went out of the Church in a body, and they were no more plagued with us in the Church. . . . My dear Lord was with us, and we were filled with fresh vigor to get a house erected to worship God in.[3]

The organization of the African Methodist Episcopal Church followed soon after.

Sometimes white northern churchmen want to distinguish their attitudes toward blacks from those of their southern brethren, suggesting that their doors have always been opened to blacks. The doors may have been opened, but only if blacks accepted their assigned places by whites. Northerners should be reminded that existence of all black independent churches among "freemen" is due exclusively to black refusal to accept the racism deeply embedded in the structure of white churches. Like southerners, white northern churchmen did not regard blacks as equals and therefore regulated the affairs of church life in the interest of white superiority. The Richard Allen episode is one example of what blacks did throughout the north. By freeing themselves from white control, blacks were able to worship God in the true spirit of the gospel, independent of the claims of white supremacy. The black church became the only sphere of black experience that was free of white power. For this reason the black church became the center for emphasis on freedom and equality. As Mays and Nicholson say: "Relatively early the church, and particularly the independent Negro church, furnished the one and only organized field in which the slave's suppressed emotions could be released, and the opportunities for him to develop his own leadership." [4]

Some black preachers, like the Rev. Highland Garnet, even urged outright rebellion against the evils of white power. He knew that appeals to "love" or "good will" would have little effect on minds warped by their own high estimation of themselves. Therefore, he taught that the spirit of liberty is a gift from God, and God thus endows the slave with the zeal to break the chains of slavery. In an address, to be sent to slaves, in 1848, at Buffalo, New York, he said:

If . . . a band of Christians should attempt to enslave a race of heathen men, and to entail slavery upon them and to keep them in heathenism in the midst of Christianity, the God of heaven would smile upon every effort which the injured might make to disenthrall themselves. Brethren, it is as wrong for your lordly oppressors to keep you in slavery as it was for the man-thief to steal our ancestors from the coast of Africa. You should therefore now use the same manner of resistance as would have been just in our ancestors when the bloody foot-prints of the first remorseless soul-thief were placed upon the shores of our fatherland. The humblest peasant is as free in the sight of God as the proudest monarch that ever swayed a sceptre. Liberty is a spirit sent from God and, like its great Author, is no respecter of persons. Brethren, the time has come when you must act for yourselves. It is an old and true saying that, "if hereditary bondmen would be free, they must themselves strike the blow." [5]

Nat Turner, a Baptist preacher and a slave, not only urged rebellion against white slaveowners, but became an ardent leader of the most successful slave revolt. He felt commissioned by God to lead slaves into a new age of freedom. In 1831, he and his group killed sixty whites in twenty-four hours before they were overpowered by state and federal troops.

While most black preachers did not take part in revolts, few failed to see that God hated slavery. For the Rev. Nathaniel Paul, God *had* to hate it, and to the point of being actively involved in its elimination. "Did I believe that it [slavery] would always continue . . . I would at once confess myself an atheist, and deny the existence of a holy God." [6] God must be against slavery, and not merely passively against it, but actively fighting to destroy it. It was impossible to believe in God and at the same time accept slavery as ordained by him.

Most black preachers were thus in a state of existential absurdity. They could not understand why God even permitted slavery. Like the biblical Job, they knew that whatever their sins or the sins of their forefathers, they did not justify slavery. The punishment did not fit the crime. Furthermore, they knew that their white oppressors were no more righteous than they. It was this contradiction which led Nathaniel Paul to ask:

Tell me, ye mighty waters, why did ye sustain the ponderous load of misery? Or speak, ye winds, and say why it was that ye executed your office to waft them onward to the still more dismal state; and ye proud waves, why did you refuse to lend your aid and to have overwhelmed them with your billows? Then should they have slept sweetly in the bosom of the great deep, and so have been hid from sorrow. And, oh thou immaculate God, be not angry with us, while we come into thy sanctuary, and make the bold inquiry in this thy holy temple, why it was that thou didst look on with calm indifference of an unconcerned spectator, when thy holy law was violated, thy divine authority despised and a portion of thine own creatures reduced to a state of mere vassalage and misery? [7]

These words sound like a Job or a Habakkuk questioning the righteousness of God. Slavery is contradictory to the character of God; it is absurd to affirm the love of God and watch men brutalized by the whips of white power. God must answer, if he expects the black man to be his servant. Therefore, Nathaniel Paul can only affirm his faith in God in view of his assurance that God hates slavery and that his righteousness prevails over evil.

Hark! While he answers from on high: hear Him proclaiming from the skies—Be still, and know that I am God! Clouds and darkness are around about me; yet righteousness and judgment are the habitation of my throne. I do my will and pleasure in the heavens above, and in the earth beneath; it is my sovereign prerogative to bring good out of evil, and cause the wrath of man to praise me, and the remainder of that wrath I will restrain.[8]

We can easily see that his view of the God of Christianity is closely tied to the present reality of this world. There is no suggestion here that the gospel is unrelated to this life. God cannot be God, a God worthy of worship and praise, and also ordain or even permit slavery. To think otherwise is to deny reality. How can we affirm his existence and believe that he permits slavery? It was this contradiction which disturbed the very "soul" of the black preachers. Belief in God was not easy for them. It was an awesome experience, burdened with responsibility. Daniel A. Payne, an A.M.E. bishop (elected in 1852) put it this way:

Sometimes it seemed as though some wild beast had plunged his fangs into my heart, and was squeezing out its life-blood. Then I began to question the existence of God, and to say: "If he does exist, is he just? If so, why does he suffer one race to oppress and enslave another, to rob them by unrighteous enactments of rights, which they hold most dear and sacred?" Sometimes I wished for the lawmakers what Nero wished—"that the Romans had but one neck." I would be the man to sever the head from its shoulders. Again said I: "Is there no God?"[9]

This agonizing experience over God's existence makes the twentieth-century death-of-God theology seem like child's play. There is something ironical about affirming God's death in view of one's identity with a cultural structure which enslaves. If the affirmation of God's death grows out of one's identity with suffering, then it is understandable, perhaps necessary. But if it arises out of one's identity with an advancing technological secular society which ignores the reality of God and the humanity of man, then it appears to be the height of human pride. This is the most disturbing fact in relation to recent developments in American white theology. Most American white Protestants who sense an identity with the death-of-God movement in Protestant theology take their cue from Dietrich Bonhoeffer. It was Bonhoeffer who said: "Honesty demands that we recognize that we live in a world as if there were no God. And this is just what we do recognize—before God! God himself drives us to this realization. God makes us know that we must live as men who can get along without Him. The God who is with us is the God who forsakes us (Mk. 15:34)! We stand continually in the presence of the God who makes us live in the world without the God-hypothesis." [10] From this and other similar quotations, some theologians have concluded that Bonhoeffer inaugurated a new age, an age of No-God. But what most white Protestant professors of theology overlook is that these are the words of a prisoner, a man who encountered the evils of Nazism and was killed in the encounter. Do whites really have the right to affirm God's death when they have actually enslaved men in God's name? It would seem that unless whites are willing to endure the pain of oppression, they cannot authentically speak of God. Relevant theology can only arise when it is unreservedly identified with the suffering of the oppressed.

It was the black preacher's unqualified identification with the black slave which created his doubts about God's existence. Similarly, it is understandable when many Black Power people shun the religion of Christianity and view God as meaningless in the black revolution. It may even be necessary, in light of white prostitution of the faith. But the black preachers during slavery did not think it necessary. They were assured that God was alive and that he was working in history against the evils of slavery. It was this assurance of which Payne spoke.

But then there came into my mind those solemn words: "with God one day is as a thousand years and a thousand years as one day. Trust in him, and he will bring slavery and all its outrages to an end." These words from the spirit world acted on my troubled soul like water on a burning fire, and my aching heart was soothed and relieved from its burden of woes.[11]

This peace of which Payne speaks is not an easy peace. It is a restless peace; it is a peace that makes him fight against human slavery, despite the odds. In a speech, delivered June, 1839, at the Franckean Synod, he said:

I am opposed to slavery, not because it enslaves the black man, but because it enslaves *man*. And were all the slaveholders in this land men of color, and the slaves white men, I would be as thorough and uncompromising an abolitionist as I now am; for whatever and whenever I may see a being in the form of a man, enslaved by his fellowman, without respect to his complexion, I shall lift my voice to plead his cause, against all the claims of his proud oppressor; and I shall do it not merely from the sympathy which man feels towards suffering man, but because *God, the living God,* whom I dare not disobey, has commanded me to open my mouth for the dumb, and to plead the cause of the oppressed.[12]

I am not unaware that many slaves accepted their condition as slaves because of the fear of white power. We may even assume that some black ministers preached that Christianity was unrelated to earthly freedom. We have already observed that most of the Spirituals are not protest songs, but a means of making a psychological adjustment to the existence of serfdom. For this reason, white slave masters believed that Christianity made the slave a better slave. In the south there were few independent black churches. Most slaves worshiped with their masters or in their own church closely supervised by "reliable" white persons. Most writers refer to church among the slaves as the "invisible institution."

It is important to note that white masters urged the slaves to worship with them and usually prohibited independent black churches. The reason is clear. The black northern independents carried the message of freedom and equality to the southern black slave, causing alarm among the white masters. "The religious congregations in the towns and the fellowship in the fields were the home base for Negro liberators, who not only preached freedom but provoked insurrections." [13] After the Nat Turner revolt, whites began to set up stricter laws to govern the behavior of the slaves. Whites realized that the black man could not be trusted to remain obedient, subservient to the will of the master, if the former was permitted to hear the gospel of the black independents or black slaves inspired with the spirit of freedom. Therefore, in order to ensure that the master's dominance over the slave would not be pre-empted by a higher will, the master prevented all instruction in religion except by authorized white persons.

In an effort to dissipate the slave's passionate desire for freedom, white missionaries sought to interpret the meaning of Christianity in the light of a futuristic eschatology, trying to convince the slave that the Christian gospel was concerned with pietistic moralities in this life as a means of gaining eternal life upon death. Thus Christianity was supposed to be concerned with the other world, what Nietzsche called "the illusion of worlds-behind-the-scene." But the black churches refused to accept an interpretation of Christianity which was unrelated to social change. They knew that though Christianity is eschatological, it must be related to the suffering of black men now. Though the black preacher looked to the future and spoke of it in heavenly terms, it was because of his vision into the future that he could never reconcile himself to the present evil of slavery. To look toward the future is to grasp the truth of God, and to grasp the truth of God is to become intolerant of untruth.

The German theologian Jürgen Moltmann has surprisingly caught the spirit of the black slave preachers. To hope in Christ means that there is "not only a consolation in suffering, but also the *protest* of *divine* promise against suffering."[14] The Christian must be assured that God is fighting against it. God must be the enemy of all those who in "sloth" put up with evil. Hope, then, as seen in the minds of the slave preachers, is not patience but impatience, not calmness but protest. As Moltmann says: "Those who hope in Christ can no longer put up with reality as it is, but begin to suffer under it, to contradict it: . . . Peace with God means conflict with the world."[15] If there is no vision of the future, we can easily reconcile ourselves with the *present*—the evil, the suffering and death. That Payne, Garnet, Paul, and others could not keep quiet in the face of the injustice of slavery rests not on their faith in man, but on God who in Christ promised wholeness. That is why they made the black church a disturbance in society.

The white missionaries sought to interpret hope in a way that made it unrelated to the present. They taught the slave that to hope means to look to heaven for a reward for being obedient to the master on earth. It meant accepting his present deplorable lot as a slave. With this view, Christian hope not only cheats the slave of the meaning of the present; it cheats God—the present reality of God and his involvement in the world on behalf of man. "As long as hope does not change the thought and action of men" in the present, it is meaningless.[16]

It would seem that black preachers before the Civil War were wiser than they have been pictured. They emphasized in word and deed the very point which is Moltmann's central thesis. On the one hand, the concept of hope is central in the preaching of black ministers. They taught their people to look to the future, to visualize a new day. And the Spirituals bear testimony to their concern for the future. On the other hand, their concern for the future did not relieve them of their responsibility for the present. Instead, it enhanced it. Through the hope which arises in Jesus, the present became intolerable. They could no longer reconcile slavery and Christianity. They heard the promise, and the promise was "incongruous with the reality around them, as they" groped "in hope towards the promised new future. The result was not the religious sanctification of the present, but a break-away from the present towards the future." [17]

Benjamin Mays and Joseph Washington have shown that for the pre-Civil War black preacher, Christianity was inextricably related to social justice in this world.[18] Washington called this concern "folk religion" and placed it outside the main stream of Christian tradition.[19] But the heretics were not the slave preachers, but white missionaries who sought to use Christianity as an instrument for enslavement. Like the early Christians who saw the difference between "law" (Judaism) and "gospel" (Christ), the black slave preachers saw that slavery and Christianity were as different as white and black. This recognition made the early black churches the center of protest against the system of slavery. It is true, as Washington suggests, that the slave preachers were virtually theologically illiterate, and even to this day few blacks have made any substantial contribution to white theology. But literacy was never a precondition to religious insight. As Hordern says, Jesus did not say, Blessed are the brilliant, but, Blessed are the pure in heart for they shall see God.

It was, rather, white Christianity in America that was born in heresy. Its very coming to be was an attempt to reconcile the impossible—slavery and Christianity. And the existence of the black churches is a visible reminder of its apostasy. The black church is the only church in America which remained recognizably Christian during pre-Civil War days. Its stand on freedom and equality through word and action is true to the spirit of Christ.

The Post-Civil War Black Church

The southern "invisible institution" among blacks became visible in a host of new black churches, united in spirit to the already existing black independents. The founding of a church was one of the ways blacks expressed their new freedom. According to Mays and Nicholson, "the freedom which the Negro felt in this period is best revealed by the fact that of the 333 rural and urban churches of this study which originated then, 231, or 69 percent came into existence through the initiative of individuals and groups." [20]

It is important to point out that the new organizations were sometimes directly related to expulsions from white churches. Here it becomes clear that white masters "accepted" black slaves in their churches as a means of keeping the black man regulated as a slave. There was no mutual relationship between equals. Therefore, when whites saw that it was no longer economically advantageous to worship with blacks, they put blacks out of their church as a matter of course. Some whites were gentle in the process, giving the blacks a plot of ground or occasionally a building for a place of worship. (That was a small price for 250 years of slavery!)

It is a credit to the humanity of black people that they recognized their presence in white services as an adjunct of slavery. Therefore, many of them left before being expelled. For this reason, we may describe the black churches during this period as a place of retreat from the dehumanizing forces of white power. It was one place in which the blacks were "safe" from the new racist structures that replaced slavery. The black church gradually became an instrument of escape instead of, as formerly, an instrument of protest.

Following the Civil War black leaders were recruited from the churches to serve in public capacities previously closed to black people. But the end of Reconstruction meant the end of black involvement in state politics. The new Jim Crow structure had devastating effects comparable to slavery. In slavery one knows what the odds are and what is needed to destroy the power of the enemy. But in a society which pronounces a man free but makes him behave as a slave, all of the strength and will power is sapped from the would-be rebel. The structures of evil are camouflaged, the enemy is elusive, and the victim is trained to accept the values of the oppressor. The "second-class citizen" is told that his oppression is due to his ignorance and his mental inferiority. At this point the oppressed is duped into believing that if only he were like the oppressor, he would no longer be ridiculed. A crash program of self-help is then devised to bridge the gap between the educated and the ignorant. This is largely the role of the black churches, the Booker T. Washingtons in the area of religion.

The black church thus lost its zeal for freedom in the midst of the new structures of white power. The rise of segregation and discrimination in the post-Civil War period softened its drive for equality. The black minister remained the spokesman for the black people, but, "faced by insurmountable obstacles, he succumbed to the cajolery and bribery of the white power structure and became its foil." [21] The passion for freedom was replaced with innocuous homilies against drinking, dancing, and smoking; and injustices in the present were minimized in favor of a Kingdom beyond this world. Black churches adopted, for the most part, the theology of the white missionaries and taught blacks to forget the present and look to the future. Some black ministers even urged blacks to adopt the morality of white society entirely, suggesting that entrance into the Kingdom of heaven is dependent on obedience to the laws of white society. A jail sentence or a fine meant that a person was immoral, subject often to churchly probation and sometimes to expulsion. Other ministers said that suffering in this life was necessary for the next life. Undue concern about white injustice was thus a sign of a loss of faith, a failure to realize that patience and long-suffering were more pertinent to final judgment than zeal for present justice. "Seek first the Kingdom of God and its righteousness and all these other things will be added unto you." This meant endurance now, liberty later.

The black minister thus became a most devoted "Uncle Tom," the transmitter of white wishes, the admonisher of obedience to the caste system. He was the liaison man between the white power structure and the oppressed blacks, serving the dual function of assuring whites that all is well in the black community, dampening the spirit of freedom among his people. More than any other one person in the black community, the black minister perpetuated the white system of black dehumanization.

The National Association for the Advancement of Colored People and the Urban League (and later the Congress of Racial Equality, the Southern Christian Leadership Conference, and the Student Nonviolent Coordinating Committee) were created because of the failure of the black church to plead the cause of black people in white society. Just as the black church is a visible reminder of the apostasy of the white church, the current civil rights protest organizations are visible manifestations of the apostasy of the black church. Forgetting their reason for existing, the black churches became, as Washington appropriately describes, "amusement centers," "arenas for power politics," and an "organ for recognition, leadership, and worship." They became perversions of the gospel of Christ and places for accommodating the oppressed plight of black people.

It was not long before the black people themselves began to recognize the failure of the black church and its ministers to speak to the needs of black people. During the Great Depression the terms of censure were characteristically blunt. St. Clair Drake and Horace R. Cayton report these criticisms of black ministers:

Blood-suckers! . . . they'll take the food out of your mouth and make you think they are doing you a favor.

You take these preachers . . . they're living like kings—got great big Packard automobiles and ten or twelve suits and a bunch of sisters putting food in their pantry. Do you call that religion? Naw! It ain't nothing but a bunch of damn monkey foolishness.[22]

Church members were almost as critical, as shown by three separate comments.

I'm a church member. I believe churches are still useful. But like everything else, there is a lot of racketeering going on in the church.

Ministers are not as conscientious as they used to be. They are money-mad nowadays. All they want is the almighty dollar and that is all they talk about.

The preachers want to line their pockets with gold. They are sup-posed to be the leaders of the people, but they are fake leaders.[23]

In all fairness to the black church and its leaders, it should be pointed out that the apostasy of the black church is partly under-standable. If they had not supported the caste system of segrega-tion and discrimination, they would have placed their lives and the lives of their people in danger. They would have been lynched and their churches burned. Thus, by cooperating with the system, they protected their lives and the lives of their people from the menacing threat of white racism. But this is not an excuse for their lack of obedience to Christ. It merely explains it.

But the real sin of the black church and its leaders is that they even convinced themselves that they were doing the right thing by advocating obedience to white oppression as a means of entering at death the future age of heavenly bliss. The black church identified white words with God's Word and convinced its people that by listening in faithful obedience to the "great white father" they would surely enter the "pearly gates." Thus the creativity of the black church which characterized the pre-Civil War period is missing after the war.

To add to this error, the black ministers received personal favors from white society. Their churches were left alone. As long as blacks preached "about heaven and told Negroes to be honest and obedient, and that by and by God would straighten things out,"[24] whites supported black churches by loaning them money to build new structures. Churches could get enormous loans and gifts from white businessmen when no other group could. Whites found that it was a good investment for the maintenance of the caste system, despite the fact that church property is useless from an economic perspective if the black people fail to repay. And the black ministers served them well. They kept the status quo intact and assured Mr. Charlie that black people were appreciative of his generosity toward the black community.

Even in the north the black church failed to maintain its freedom from white controls. The criticisms cited from Drake and Cayton on the black church were made by people from Chicago. Like southern black ministers, they too emphasized white moralities as a means of entrance in God's future Kingdom. Few black northern churches joined the oppressed blacks by challenging the existing white power structure.[25] Generally, they pursued worldly matters with the major emphasis on the "almighty dollar" for personal use.

We may conclude that except in rare instances, the black churches in the post-Civil War period have been no more Christian than their white counterparts. The rare instances refer chiefly to the recent work of a few black ministers in the non-violent movement, with the late Martin Luther King, Jr., as their leader. At least during its early stages this movement was a return to the spirit of the pre-Civil War black preachers with the emphasis being on freedom and equality in the present political structure. King saw clearly the meaning of the gospel with its social implications and sought to instill its true spirit in the hearts and minds of black and white in this land. He was a man endowed with the charisma of God; he was a prophet in our own time. And like no other black or white American he could set black people's hearts on fire with the gospel of freedom in Christ which would make them willing to give all for the cause of black humanity. Like the prophets of old, he had a dream, a dream grounded not in the hopes of white America but in God. Nor did the dream of the future relieve him of responsibilities in the present; instead, it made him fight unto death in order to make his dream a reality.

It may appear that white America made his dream into a

nightmare by setting the climate for his assassination and later memorializing his name with meaningless pieties. But his dream was grounded in God, not man. It was this realization that caused him to say the night before his death: "I've been on the mountain top." Like Moses he did not see the promised land but retained the unshakable certainty that God's righteousness will triumph.

Because of King's work we are now in the beginning stages of real confrontation between black and white Americans. He may not have endorsed the concept of Black Power, but its existence is a result of his work. Black Power advocates are men who were inspired by his zeal for freedom, and Black Power is their attempt to make his dream a reality. If the black church organizations want to remain faithful to the New Testament gospel and to the great tradition of the pre-Civil War black church, they must relinquish their stake in the status quo and the values in white society by identifying exclusively with Black Power. Black Power is the only hope of the black church in America.

Some black ministers are beginning to catch the spirit of Black Power and are seeking to embrace it. A case in point is the group of some 250 black Methodists who met in Cincinnati in February, 1968, in order to assess their place in the United Methodist Church and their role in the black revolution. In "The Black Paper," they began with a confession:

We, a group of black Methodists in America, are deeply disturbed about the crisis of racism in America. We are equally concerned about the failure of a number of black people, including black Methodists, to respond appropriately to the roots and forces of racism and the current Black Revolution.

We, as black Methodists, must first respond in a state of confession because it is only as we confront ourselves that we are able to deal with the evils and forces which seek to deny our humanity.

We confess our failure to be reconciled with ourselves as black men. We have too often denied our blackness (hair texture, color and other God-given physical characteristics) rather than embrace it in all its black beauty.

We confess that we have not always been relevant in service and ministry to our black brothers, and in so doing we have alienated ourselves from many of them.

We confess that we have not always been honest with ourselves and with our white brothers. We have not encountered them with truth but often with deception. We have not said in bold language and forceful action that, "You have used 'white power' in and outside of the church to keep us in a subordinate position." We have failed to tell our white brothers "like it is!" Instead, we have told our white brothers what we *thought* they would like to hear.

We confess that we have not become significantly involved in the Black Revolution because, for the most part, white men have defined it as "bad"; for the other part, we have been too comfortable in our "little world," and too pleased with our lot as second-class citizens and second-class members of The Methodist Church.

We confess that we have accepted too long the philosophy of racism. This has created a relationship in which white people have always defined the "terms," and, in fact, defined when and how black people would exist.

We confess that we have accepted a "false kind of integration" in which all power remained in the hands of white men.[26]

They not only confessed but emphasized that the embracing of Black Power is the only meaningful response "to racism in America and racism in The United Methodist Church." They said: "It [Black Power] is a call for us to respond to God's action in history which is to make and keep human life human."[27] The black Methodists went on to outline a beginning program for black and white churches interested in making a relevant response to the Black Power revolution.

Another sign of hope in black churches occurred when several leaders of many denominations issued a statement on "Black Power" in 1966.[28] While they failed to endorse the concept of Black Power as a working concept,[29] as did the "Black Methodists for Church Renewal," they did stress the fact that white racism is the basic reason for black unrest in America. And they also recognized that "powerlessness breeds a race of beggars."

But we must warn our black churchmen that there are dangers in making confessions and writing papers. It is so easy to think that a careful, rational articulation of the problem means that the oppressor will concede and cease his work of dehumanization. But the evaluation of the problem is merely the first step in problem-solving. The black church must be willing to proceed with a concentrated attack on the evils of racism. It also must realize that the war is not over because one battle is won. The fight against injustice is never over until all men, regardless of physical characteristics, are recognized and treated as human beings. When that happens, we can be certain that God's Kingdom has come on earth.

It seems that some black churchmen are beginning to realize the importance of backing one's resolutions with relevant action. It was heartwarming to hear that the "Black Methodists for Church Renewal" walked out of the Methodist General Conference at the moment of the communion celebrating the new United Methodist Church, in order to witness to the brokenness of the Methodist community. But one must be willing to do more than leave during communion. A more forceful confrontation is evidently necessary. It may be that black Methodists and their brothers elsewhere will need to confront churches with what is required to destroy ecclesiastical racism and be prepared to withdraw unless their demands are met. It is time for the Church to be relevant by joining Christ in the black revolution. Unless the black church is prepared to respond to Christ's command of obedience by becoming one with the unwanted, then it, like its white counterpart, is useless as a vehicle for divine reconciliation.

Some may think these criticisms are too harsh and fail to point to the basic value of the black church in the black community. Some black churchmen may want to argue that the Church, because it is owned by blacks, is important in giving many black people a sense of "somebodyness" in a hostile white world. It is the black church which bestows a sense of worth on many "common" blacks because the barriers encountered in society as a whole disappear in the Church. Therefore, the Church provides an opportunity for the common man (maid, truck driver, etc.) to explore his abilities. For this reason, it is not uncommon to find the educator and the laborer on the same church board, and often the latter is the chairman. The black church provides an opportunity for self-expression, a freedom to relax, and release from the daily grind of white racism. Is this not enough to warrant the existence of the black church?

It may warrant its existence but not in Christ. The existence of *the* Church is grounded exclusively in Christ. And in twentieth-century America, *Christ means Black Power!* It is certainly the case that the major institutional black churches have not caught the spirit of Black Power. They have, for the most part, strayed from their calling, seeking instead to pattern their life after white models. The divinely appointed task of proclaiming freedom and equality was abandoned in the ungodly pursuit of whiteness. Joseph Washington puts it graphically: "Heretofore, the function of the Negro Church has been that of a haven. In effect it has served as a cut-rate outlet, selling itself for quantity rather than quality, offering cheap white medicine in colored doses of several hours of relief for a week-long headache." [30] The only hope for the black church is to repent by seeking the true mission of Christ in the world.

It is clear that there are creative possibilities in the black church which seem to be absent in its white counterpart. The black church has a heritage of radical involvement in the world. This past is a symbol of what is actually needed in the present. The white American Church has no history of obedience; and without it, it is unlikely that it will ever know what radical obedience to Christ means. Since it is identified with the structure of power, it will always be possible for it to hedge and qualify its obedience to Christ. Also, being white in soul and mind, the white church must make a "special" effort in order to identify with the suffering of the oppressed, an effort which is almost inevitably distorted into plantation charity. To follow the line of least resistance means that it cannot be for Christ. It seems that the major white church institutions have followed that course so long that the probability is slight that they can free themselves from the structures of power in this society.

The black church, on the other hand, by virtue of being black, is automatically a part of the unwanted. It knows the meaning of rejection because it was rejected. All the black church has to do is to accept its role as the sufferer and begin to follow the natural course of being black. In so doing, it may not only redeem itself through God's Spirit, but the white church as well. The black church, then, is probably the only hope for renewal or, more appropriately, revolution in organized Christianity. It alone has attempted to be recognizably Christian in a hostile environment. It alone, being victimized by color, has championed the cause of the oppressed black people. Black churchmen are in a position to reaffirm this heritage, accepting the meaning of blackness in a white society and incorporating it into the language and work of the gospel. Speaking a true language of black liberation, the black church must teach that, in a white world bent on dehumanizing black people, Christian love means giving no ground to the enemy, but relentlessly insisting on one's dignity as a person. Love is not passive, but active. It is revolutionary in that it seeks to meet the needs of the neighbor amid crumbling structures of society. It is revolutionary because love may mean joining a violent rebellion.

The black church must ask about its function amid the rebellion of black people in America. Where does it stand? If it is to be relevant, it must no longer admonish its people to be "nice" to white society. It cannot condemn the rioters. It must make an unqualified identification with the "looters" and "rioters," recognizing that this stance leads to condemnation by the state as law-breakers. There is no place for "nice Negroes" who are so distorted by white values that they regard laws as more sacred than human life. There is no place for those who deplore black violence and overlook the daily violence of whites. There is no place for blacks who want to be "safe," for Christ did not promise security but suffering.

The pre-Civil War black ministers had no trouble breaking the law when they saw human life at stake. It was beside the question whether slavery was lawful. The question was, Is it consistent with the gospel? If not, they must fight it until death. It was this realization which inspired Martin Luther King to engage in his program of civil disobedience.

So far, the black church has remained conspicuously silent, continuing its business as usual. The holding of conferences, the election of bishops, the fund-raising drive for a new building or air-conditioner seem to be more important than the blacks who are shot because they want to be men. The black church, though spatially located in the community of the oppressed, has not responded to the needs of its people. It has, rather, drained the community, seeking to be more and more like the white church. Its ministers have condemned the helpless and have mimicked the values of whites. For this reason most Black Power people bypass the churches as irrelevant to their objectives.

Today we enter a new era, the era of Black Power. It is an age of rebellion and revolution. Blacks are no longer prepared to turn the other cheek; instead, they are turning the gun. Blacks are dying in the streets at the hands of hired gunmen of the state because they refuse to respond to white oppression. This is an era when many blacks would rather die than be slaves. Now the question is: What do the black churches have to say about this? It is time for the black churches to change their style and join the suffering of the black masses, proclaiming the gospel of the black Christ. Whether they will do this is not clear now. What is clear is that they are poised at the moment of irrevocable decision, between costly obedience and confirmed apostasy.

It is hard to know whether to laugh or weep as the churches make bargains with the principalities and powers: prayers on public occasions, tax exemptions, shying away from vital issues, exhortations to private goodness, promotion of gutless "spirituality," institutional self-glorification—they are all knotted together in a monstrous ungodly tangle that spells death to black humanity. There is, of course, a difference between white churches and black churches. But the similarities are striking. Both have marked out their places as havens of retreat, the one to cover the guilt of the oppressors, the other to daub the wounds of the oppressed. Neither is notably identified with the tearing-healing power of Christ. Neither is a fit instrument of revolution.

In such a situation the idea of "renewal" seems futile. Renewal suggests that there is a core of healthy, truthful substance under all the dirt and rust. But dirt can grind away a delicate mechanism, and rust can consume rather than merely cover. The white church in America, though occasionally speaking well and even more rarely acting well, generally has been and is the embodiment of what is wrong with the society. It is racism in ecclesiastical robes. It lives and breathes bigotry. The black church embodies a response to racism at the level of sheer survival at the price of freedom and dignity. Both have taken the road marked "the good life," avoiding the call to discipleship, which is the call to suffering and death. For this reason, renewal in any ordinary sense seems out of the question.

V

Some Perspectives
of Black Theology

Show the chains. Let them see the chains as
object and subject, and let them see
the chains fall away.

LeRoi Jones

Just as the black revolution means the death of America as it
has been, so it requires the death of the Church in its familiar
patterns. The sixteenth-century radical concept of the "restoration of the church" is more appropriate to our times than the
idea of renewal. But there is no need to quibble over slogans.
What is meant is that the life of the Church of Christ is life
out of death, the resurrection of bleached and windswept bones.

Black religionists must begin serious thinking about the meaning of Christian obedience in an age of black revolution. We
need a theology for the oppressed black people of America aimed
at the destruction of racism in the society. Black theologians
can no longer be tied to the irrelevancies of white American
"Christianity."

The Rev. Albert Cleage of Detroit is one of the few black
ministers who has embraced Black Power as a religious concept
and has sought to reorient the church-community on the basis
of it. The Black Muslims, through allegiance to Islam, have dem-

onstrated more than any existing black religious community, the relationship between religion and the suffering of black people. It is time for black Christian theologians to begin to relate Christianity to the pain of being black in a white racist society, or else Christianity itself will be discarded as irrelevant in its perverse whiteness. Christianity needs remaking in the light of black oppression. In this chapter I will endeavor to set forth some basic perspectives of Black Theology.

On Black Suffering

Black Theology must take seriously the reality of black people—their life of suffering and humiliation. This must be the point of departure of all God-talk which seeks to be black-talk. When that man is black and lives in a society permeated with white racist power, he can speak of God only from the perspective of the socio-economic and political conditions unique to black people. Though the Christian doctrine of God must logically precede the doctrine of man, Black Theology knows that black people can view God only through black eyes that behold the brutalities of white racism. To ask them to assume a "higher" identity by denying their blackness is to require them to accept a false identity and to reject reality as they know it to be.

The task of Black Theology, then, is *to analyze the black man's condition in the light of God's revelation in Jesus Christ with the purpose of creating a new understanding of black dignity among black people, and providing the necessary soul in that people, to destroy white racism.* Black Theology is primarily a theology *of* and *for* black people who share the common belief that racism will be destroyed only when black people decide to say in word and deed to the white racist: "We ain't gonna stand any more of this." The purpose of Black Theology is to analyze the nature of the Christian faith in such a way that black people can say Yes to blackness and No to whiteness and mean it.

It is not the purpose of Black Theology to address white people, at least not directly. Though whites may read it, understand it, and even find some meaning in it, Black Theology is not dependent on white perception. It assumes that the possibilities of creative response among white people to black humiliation are virtually nonexistent. What slim possibilities there are belong only to those whites who are wholly committed to the activity of destroying racism in the structure of the white community. The goal of Black Theology is to prepare the minds of blacks for freedom so that they will be ready to give all for it. Black Theology must speak *to* and *for* black people as they seek to remove the structures of white power which hover over their being, stripping it of its blackness.

Because Black Theology has as its starting point the black condition, this does not mean that it denies the absolute revelation of God in Christ. Rather, it means that Black Theology firmly believes that God's revelation in Christ can be made supreme only by affirming Christ as he is alive in black people today. Black Theology is Christian theology precisely because it has the black predicament as its point of departure. It calls upon black people to affirm God because he has affirmed us. His affirmation of black people is made known not only in his election of oppressed Israel, but more especially in his coming to us and being rejected in Christ for us. The event of Christ tells us that the oppressed blacks are his people because, and only because, they represent who he is.

On Religious Authority

The question of authority has been and still is in some circles a much-debated religious question. Protestant Christianity was born because Martin Luther denied the absolute authority of the Pope in religious matters.

Ultimate and absolute authority in matters of faith can and must reside only in the Word of God, who was made flesh, died and rose again for our salvation, and abides for ever in His Church. In Him and through Him God has spoken to men; here only have we the unmistakable voice of God, unimpeded in its utterance by the weakness of sinful nature and the fallibility of sinful human thought.[1]

For Luther, Christ alone is supreme authority and the Scripture is second only to Christ.

Within Protestantism, liberalism, fundamentalism, and neo-orthodoxy[2] have exerted much time and energy discussing the question. Fundamentalists (sometimes referred to as conservatives) emphasize the verbal inspiration of Scripture and locate final authority in the infallibility of the text itself. The Scripture is God's Word in that "by a special, supernatural, extraordinary influence of the Holy Ghost, the sacred writers have been guided in their writing in such a way, as while their humanity was not superseded it was yet so dominated that their words became at the same time the words of God, and thus, in every case and all alike, infallible."[3] Liberals would be much freer in their treatment of the Bible. Certainly they would not agree that the Scripture is infallible or is the supreme authority on matters of faith. They would be more inclined to emphasize the place of *reason* in matters of faith and life. The neo-orthodox theologians would emphasize the authority of God's disclosure of himself in Jesus Christ. They seem to represent the Reformation theology of the sixteenth century as expressed in Luther and Calvin.

In more recent times, the question of religious authority is not discussed in the way it used to be. In the past (especially among the fundamentalists, liberals, and neo-orthodox theologians), it was essentially a private debate among religious scholars abstracted from real life in the world. Politically, in America at least, it did not matter whose side one supported. None of the positions threatened the basic structure of the nation. Now, however, religious thinkers have begun to relate theological talk to worldly talk, and some have even begun to question the way men live in the society. This is clearly seen in writings of William Sloane Coffin, Jr., the Yale University chaplain; he not only wrote about it but acted in such a manner that he was tried, convicted, and sentenced for his "illegal" draft counseling. In a less dramatic fashion, the rise of the death-of-God theology means that religious authority not only involves one's participation in a churchly community but equally in the secular community.

It is within this larger context of "the world" that we are to understand Black Theology and religious authority. The discussion of authority must depart from the abstract debate among fundamentalist, liberalist, and neo-orthodox thinkers. Though there are expressions of these three major streams of Protestant thought within the black churches, Black Theology sees a prior authority that unites all black people and transcends these theological differences. It is this common experience among black people in America that Black Theology elevates as the supreme test of truth. To put it simply, Black Theology knows no authority more binding than the experience of oppression itself. This alone must be the ultimate authority in religious matters.

Concretely, this means that Black Theology is not prepared to accept any doctrine of God, man, Christ, or Scripture which contradicts the black demand for freedom now. It believes that any religious idea which exalts black dignity and creates a restless drive for freedom must be affirmed. All ideas which are opposed to the struggle for black self-determination or are irrelevant to it must be rejected as the work of the Antichrist.

Again, this does not mean that Black Theology makes the experience of Christ secondary to the experience of black oppression. Rather, it means that black people have come to know Christ precisely through oppression, because he has made himself synonymous with black oppression. Therefore, to deny the reality of black oppression and to affirm some other "reality" is to deny Christ. Through Christ, black people have come to know not only who he is but also who they are, and what they must do about that which would make them nothings. When the question is asked, "On what authority, in the last resort, do we base our claim that this or that doctrine is part of the Gospel and therefore true?" [4] Black Theology must say: "If the doctrine is compatible with or enhances the drive for black freedom, then it is the gospel of Jesus Christ. If the doctrine is against or indifferent to the essence of blackness as expressed in Black Power, then it is the work of the Antichrist." It is as simple as that.

Black Theology is not prepared to discuss the doctrine of God, man, Christ, Church, Holy Spirit—the whole spectrum of Christian theology—without making each doctrine an analysis of the emancipation of black people. It believes that, in this time, moment, and situation, all Christian doctrines must be interpreted in such a manner that they unreservedly say something to black people who are living under unbearable oppression.

On Eschatology

The most corrupting influence among the black churches was their adoption of the "white lie" that Christianity is primarily concerned with an otherworldly reality. White missionaries persuaded most black religious people that life on earth was insignificant because obedient servants of God could expect a "reward" in heaven after death. As one might expect, obedience meant adherence to the laws of the white masters. Most black people accepted the white interpretation of Christianity, which divested them of the concern they might have had about their freedom in the present. Even a casual look at the black Spirituals shows their otherworldly character.

> O Lawd, when I die,
> I want to go to heav'n
> My Lord, when I die.

You'd better min'
You'd better min'
For you got to give account in Judgment,
You'd better min'.

Others, such as, "Religion Is a Fortune I Really Do Believe," "By an' By," "All God's Chilluns Got Wings," "Get on Board, Little Chillen," and "Give Me Jesus," reveal the same mood.

This otherworldly ethos is still very much a part of the black churches. This is not merely a problem of education among the black clergy; mainly it shows that white power is so overwhelming in its domination of black people that many blacks have given up hope for change in this world. By reaching for heaven they are saying that the odds are against them now; God must have something better in store for black people later. That is why a great many black preachers say:

Heaven is my home and I am homesick. There I will meet all the saints who have gone on before me. My mother and father will be there in that great host. I want to see them again. I want to look into the eyes of Abraham, take a long walk with Moses, talk with Ruth, feel the arms of Esau, and shake Jacob by the hand. There I will have the chance to ask Jacob about his suffering, thank the prophets for their courage, and sit beside Lazarus. Above all, I want to be with Jesus of Galilee: my Lord and my God. There will be no more crying up there, no pain up there, no second-class citizenship up there. There will be nothing but peace in God's Kingdom. Up there, I will have a time.[5]

The contrast between white treatment of black people as things and God's view of them as persons is so great that it is easy for blacks to think that God has withdrawn from history and the "devil" has taken over. Black people begin to affirm that if one has "Jesus," it does not matter whether there is injustice, brutality, and suffering. Jesus thus becomes a magical name which gives the people a distorted hope in another life. Through identification with a name, unbearable suffering becomes bearable.

Instead of seeking to change the earthly state, they focus their hopes on the next life in heaven. In reality, this is not the perspective of the biblical faith but, rather, an expression of a hopeless faith which cannot come to terms with the reality of this world.

Understandably, most black intellectuals reject this attitude, especially the advocates of Black Power. As one black man put it: "The black man stood on the corner and said, 'take the world and give me Jesus.' So that's just what the white man did. 'Jesus will help us' the black man said. Hell, Jesus couldn't even help his own self. He fooled around and got himself nailed to the cross." [6] There is certainly something to be said for the idea that any concept of God which defines him as removed from the suffering of black people now cannot win the devotion of the new black man. The passive acceptance of injustice is not the way of human beings.

If eschatology means that one believes that God is totally uninvolved in the suffering of men because he is preparing them for another world, then Black Theology is not eschatological. Black Theology is an earthly theology! It is not concerned with the "last things" but with the "white thing." Black Theology like Black Power believes that the self-determination of black people must be emphasized at all costs, recognizing that there is only one question about reality for blacks: What must we do about white racism? There is no room in this perspective for an eschatology dealing with a "reward" in heaven. Black Theology has hope for this life. The appeal to the next life is a lack of hope. Such an appeal implies that absurdity has won and that one is left merely with an unrealistic gesture toward the future. Heavenly hope becomes a Platonic grasp for another reality because one cannot live meaningfully amid the suffering of this world.

In traditional eschatology, suffering is often interpreted as the means for heavenly entrance. "Blessed are those who are persecuted for righteousness' sake, for theirs is the Kingdom of heaven. Blessed are you when men revile you and persecute you and utter all kinds of evil against you falsely on my account. Rejoice and be glad, for your reward is great in heaven, for so men persecuted the prophets who were before you" (Matt. 5:10–12). Evil and injustice are transformed into temporary good in view of the apocalypse. Black Theology rejects this interpretation, sharing instead the viewpoint of Dr. Rieux in Camus's *The Plague*. During the height of the plague in the Algerian city of Oran, Rieux, Father Paneloux, and others witness the prolonged death agony of a child. A moment after the child dies, Rieux rushes from the room, a bewildered look on his face, and Paneloux tries to stop him. Rieux turns fiercely to Paneloux: "Ah, that child, anyhow, was innocent, and you know it as well as I do!" Rieux goes outside and sits on a bench. Paneloux joins him.

"Why was there that anger in your voice just now? What we'd been seeing was as unbearable to me as it was to you."

Rieux turned toward Paneloux.

"I know. I'm sorry. But weariness is a kind of madness. And there are times when the only feeling I have is one of mad revolt."

"I understand," Paneloux said in a low voice. "That sort of thing is revolting because it passes our human understanding. But perhaps we should love what we cannot understand."

Rieux straightened up slowly. He gazed at Paneloux, summoning to his gaze all the strength and fervor he could muster against his weariness. Then he shook his head.

"No, Father, I've a very different idea of love. And until my dying day I shall refuse to love a scheme of things in which children are put to torture." [7]

This is the key to Black Theology. It refuses to embrace any concept of God which makes black suffering the will of God. Black people should not accept slavery, lynching, or any form of injustice as tending to good. It is not permissible to appeal to the idea that God's will is inscrutable or that the righteous sufferer will be rewarded in heaven. If God has made the world in which black people *must* suffer, and if he is a God who rules, guides, and sanctifies the world, then he is a murderer. To be the God of black people, he must be against the oppression of black people.

The idea of heaven is irrelevant for Black Theology. The Christian cannot waste time contemplating the next world (if there is a next). Radical obedience to Christ means that reward cannot be the motive for action. It is a denial of faith to insist on the relevance of reward. Is this not what St. Paul had in mind when he spoke of justification? When Paul uses the term "justification" in reference to Christ he means that sinful man, through complete trust alone, is accepted by God and is declared and treated as a righteous man. He is emphasizing man's inability to make himself righteous. All human strivings are nil; man cannot earn God's acceptance (Rom. 3:20, 23; Gal. 3:22). Salvation is by the free grace of God. There is no place for the conceit that men can save themselves by their own efforts, if they try hard enough. The Incarnation means that man stands unworthy before God. "Man is helpless under God's wrath, but God is not only just in condemning and punishing sin; he is so completely just that he also provides a means of deliverance from sin, giving freely what man could never achieve for himself." [8]

There is no place here for a reward. In fact, man is now made free for obedience without worrying about a pat on the back from God. He now knows that he is right with God because God has put him in the right. This new gift of freedom means that he can be all for the neighbor. To allow one's concern to be directed toward heaven is to deny the freedom. It means that in some way what one does *is* worthy and thereby guarantees his favor with God. The free Christian man cannot be concerned about a reward in heaven. Rather, he is a man who, through the freedom granted in Christ, is ready to plunge himself into the evils of the world, revolting against all inhuman powers which enslave men. He does not seek salvation, for he knows that to seek it is to lose it. "He that would save his life will lose it. He who loses his life for my sake will gain it." He is a rebel against inhumanity and injustice.

Black Theology rejects the tendency of some to interpret eschatology in such a way that a cleavage is made between our world and God's. Black Theology insists that genuine biblical faith relates eschatology to history, that is, to what God has done, is doing, and will do for his people. It is only because of what God has done and is now doing that we can speak meaningfully of the future.

With a black perspective, eschatology comes to mean joining the world and making it what it ought to be. It means that the Christian man looks to the future not for a reward or possible punishment of evildoers, but as a means of making him dissatisfied with the present. His only purpose for looking to a distant past or an unrealized future is that both disclose the ungodliness of the present. Looking to the future he sees that present injustice cannot be tolerated. Black Theology asserts an eschatology that confronts a world of racism with Black Power. Eschatology "does not mean merely salvation of the soul, individual rescue from the evil world, comfort for the troubled conscience, but also the realization of the eschatological *hope of justice,* the *humanizing* of man, the *socializing* of humanity, *peace* for all creation." [9] Our future expectations must be turned into present realities. " 'Creative discipleship' cannot consist in adaptation to, or preservation of, the existing social and judicial orders, still less can it supply religious backgrounds for a given or manufactured situation." [10] It must consist in analyzing the present structure of things, seeking to overthrow all inhuman and unjustifiable acts of oppression. " 'Creative discipleship' of this kind in a love which institutes community, sets things right and puts them in order, becomes eschatologically possible through the Christian hope's prospects of the future of God's Kingdom and of man." [11]

Therefore hope is not a theoretical concept to be answered in a seminary classroom or in the privacy of one's experiences. It is a practical idea which deals with the reality of this world. In short, Black Theology refuses to embrace an interpretation of eschatology which would turn our eyes from injustice now. It will not be deceived by images of pearly gates and golden streets, because too many earthly streets are covered with black blood.

On the Creation of New Values

To carve out a Black Theology based on black oppression will of necessity mean the creation of new values independent of and alien to the values of white society. The values must be independent because they must arise from the needs of black people. They will be alien because white American "Christian" values are based on racism.

The call for a new value-system is not new in the history of mankind. An appropriate example is Nietzsche's demand for a "revaluation of all values," which for him meant a destruction of Christianity and the death of God. He was appalled not merely at the nature of the faith itself and its contradiction of the basic nature of man; but more importantly, he was sickened at seeing "priests," "theologians," and others who used the name "Christian" as a description of their lives, conducting themselves in contradiction to Christianity.

What was formerly just sick is today indecent—it is indecent to be a Christian today. *And here begins my nausea.* I look around: not one word has remained of what was formerly called "truth"; . . . If we have the smallest claim to integrity, we must know today that a theologian, a priest, a pope, not merely is wrong in every sentence he speaks, but lies. . . . The priest knows as well as anybody else that there is no longer any 'God,' any 'sinner,' any 'Redeemer.' . . . Everybody knows this, *and yet everything continues as before.* Where has the last feeling of decency and self-respect gone when even our statesmen, an otherwise quite unembarrassed type of man, anti-Christians through and through in their deeds, still call themselves Christians today and attend communion? [12]

From this Nietzsche concludes (perhaps rightly) that "there was only *one* Christian, and he died on the cross." [13] What is needed, according to Nietzsche, is a new set of values to be created by man himself because God is dead and the churches are nothing but "the tombs and sepulchres of God." [14]

Taking the cue from Nietzsche and other radical religionists, the term "secular" has become the watchword for many twentieth-century theologians. For some, "secular" means simply embracing the secular world (Harvey Cox); for others it implies a denial of God himself (Hamilton and Altizer); and in other segments of American theology, it symbolizes a call for an underground church and theology (Malcolm Boyd).

One positive note arising from these views of Christianity and the world is a recognition of the need for the abandoning of the institutional church. According to Boyd, the underground church is a fellowship of "unemployables" in the institutional church who are seeking to be Christian in an age of societal dehumanization. They bypass the structures of church power because they believe that suffering is more vital than saving face. In some cases, they "are participating, with thanksgiving, in the dying and in *the willing of the death*" [15] of the church. Quoting from Henri Perrin's *Priest-Workman in Germany,* Malcolm Boyd describes the spirit of the underground church:

All this calls for men who can get out of themselves, who will cease walking by lonely paths, and will come to the high roads where men of all nations pass by. Such Christians as these, leaping over the rottenness of the world at a bound, will stand up before men, bearing the light of Christ past the winding ways and false mysticisms which mislead them. This also calls for men to leave the Ghetto in which they so often shut themselves up—in *our* churches, *our* papers, *our* movements, *our* good works—this calls for them to be amongst pagans, and really become theirs as Christ became ours, giving up their life, their time, their resources, their activity, for those who haven't heard the "good tidings." A Christian hasn't finished his job when he has gone to Mass on Sunday. The Church's prayer, the body of Christ, are only given to him as a help towards bringing *him* to the world. And if men do not recognize in us the love and goodness of our Father, then we have done *nothing*—we haven't even begun to serve Him.[16]

Words like these could inspire white men to live a life-style properly called Christianity. The underground church seems to be a body of men who are seeking to be Christians independent of the organized church. According to Boyd, it is not a denial of Christianity but its affirmation. It seeks "to insist, by whatever means, that the church be itself."[17]

For whites who are concerned about Christianity and their role amid the black revolution, the underground church may be an appealing and useful style. This does not mean that they would evade the hostility of black Americans. That simply is not possible! Neither does it mean that they would avoid compromise, becoming "pure" in contrast to the corrupt establishment. "It is hard to know," writes Boyd, "what constitutes compromise. One is a social being, absorbed in social actions, and therefore the giver and receiver of moral ambiguities. What could 'dropping out' possibly mean? There is no where to go. This at least precludes a stance of self-righteousness."[18] But this does mean that even white men, despite their guilt, can define clearly, emotionally, and intellectually, what they can and cannot endure. They will not know what it means to face the reality of alienation and death, until they stop defining their existence according to the expectations of the establishment.

But for black people, the call for a new value-system must not be identified with Nietzsche, the death-of-God theology, or even the underground church. When Black Theology calls for a new value-system, it is oriented in a single direction: the bringing to bear of the spirit of black self-determination upon the consciousness of black people. It is the creation of a new cultural ethos among the oppressed blacks of America, so that they are no longer dependent on the white oppressor for their understanding of truth, reality, or—and this is the key—what ought to be done about the place of black sufferers in America. Black religion and black people can never become what they ought to be (a religion and a people unreservedly devoted to the emancipation of all blacks) as long as the content of religion is a distorted reflection of the religion of the enslaver. To be free means to be free to create new possibilities for existence.

Black theologians owe this insight to the pre-Civil War black preachers and the emergence of the Black Power concept. The black preachers of the pre-Civil War period saw the need for independent black churches whose reason for existence was to create the spirit of freedom among black people. The connection between Christianity and civil freedom was absent in most white views of Christianity. And if Black Power means anything, it means a call for black unity even in religion (especially religion!) because it realizes that only blacks can set the limits of their existence. It means that whites cannot assist in this because they too, in spite of their "good" intentions, are immersed in the total structure of racism. At most, whites can only leave blacks alone.

Black Power and black religion are inseparable. Both seek to free black people from white racism. It is impossible for Black Power to be effective without taking into consideration man's religious nature. It is impossible for black religion to be truly related to the condition of black people and to the message of Jesus Christ without emphasizing the basic tenets of Black Power. Therefore, Black Theology seeks to make black religion a religion of Black Power. It does not attempt to destroy Christianity but endeavors to point to its blackness. The task of Black Theology is to make Christianity *really* Christian by moving black people with a spirit of black dignity and self-determination so they can become what the Creator intended.

Black Theology is a theology of the black community and is

thus opposed to any idea which alienates it from that community. Since it seeks to interpret Black Power religiously, Black Theology endeavors to reorder the Christian tradition in view of the black predicament and to destroy the influence of heretical white American Christianity. In this sense, it is nationalistic. It attempts to provide black people with a sense of nationhood, knowing that until black unity is attained, black people will have no weapon against white racism.

The religious ideas of the oppressor are detrimental to the black people's drive for freedom. They tend to make black people nonviolent and accept only the prescribed patterns of protest defined by the oppressor himself. It is the oppressor who attempts to tell black people what is and is not Christian—though he is the least qualified to make such a judgment. It is he, through the news media and other forms of communication, who tries to select the "good Negro" as the leader for black people—"religious" and "secular." But Black Theology, like Black Power, rejects leaders who merely mimic the values of a racist society. Black Theology advocates a religious system of values based on the experiences of the oppressed because it believes white values must either be revolutionized or eliminated.

Such a value-system means, of course, an end to the influence of white seminaries with their middle-class white ideas about God, Christ, and the Church. This does not necessarily mean burning of their buildings with Molotov cocktails. What is meant is a removal of the oppressive ideas from the black community which the seminaries perpetuate. We must replace them with black consciousness—that is, with Nathaniel Paul, Daniel Payne, Nat Turner (not Styron's), Marcus Garvey, Elijah Muhammad, and Malcolm X. Instead of having courses dealing with the theology of Reinhold Niebuhr or Rudolf Bultmann or Emil Brunner, we need to deal with the theology of Henry Garnet and other black revolutionaries.

Black Theology seeks to do in religion what LeRoi Jones, Larry Neal, Ron Karenga, and others have done in their specialized fields. Defining Black Power, Jones says: "Black Power is the Power first to be Black." [19] But it is also "a culture, a way of feeling, a way of living, that is replaced with a culture, feeling, way of living and being, that is black, and, yes, finally, more admirable." [20] Karenga speaks of the same concern: "We stress culture because it gives identity, purpose, and direction. It tells who we are, what we must do, and how we can do it." [21] He goes on to suggest that "culture is the basis of all ideas, images, and actions. To move is to move culturally, i.e., by a set of values given to you by your culture." [22] The basic criteria for culture, according to Karenga, are mythology, history, social organization, political organization, creative motif, and ethos.[23] Larry Neal, another black artist, speaks of a "black aesthetic":

It consists of an African-American cultural tradition. . . . It encompasses most of the usable elements of Third World culture. The motive behind the Black Aesthetic is the destruction of the white thing, the destruction of white ideas, and white ways of looking at the world. The new aesthetic is mostly predicated on an Ethics which asks the question: whose vision of the world is finally more meaningful, ours or the white oppressor's? What is truth? Or more precisely, whose truth shall we express, that of the oppressed or of the oppressors? [24]

Neal further describes the meaning of the "black aesthetic" by quoting Brother Knight:

Unless the Black artist establishes a "Black aesthetic" he will have no future at all. To accept the white aesthetic is to accept and validate a society that will not allow him to live. The Black artist must create new forms and new values, sing new songs (or purify old ones); and along with other Black authorities, he must create a new history, new symbols, myths and legends. . . . And the Black artist, in creating his own aesthetic, must be accountable for it only to the Black people.[25]

It would seem that the intellectuals (not only people who read and write books but all those capable of creative thought) in the black religious community must begin the task of creating a new cultural base in order to win the minds of the black masses. LeRoi Jones's plays, *Dutchman* and *The Slave,* are examples of this for the black theater. Jones speaks to the condition of black people by describing the reality of the "white thing" as it appears to them in the American society.

Our theatre will show victims so that their brothers in the audience will be better able to understand that they are the brothers of victims, and that they themselves are victims if they are blood brothers. And what we show must cause the blood to rush, so that prerevolutionary temperaments will be bathed in this blood, and it will cause their deepest souls to move, and they will find themselves tensed and clenched, even ready to die, at what the soul has been taught. We will scream and cry, murder, run through the streets in agony, if it means some soul will be moved, moved to actual life understanding of what the world is, and what it ought to be. We are preaching virtue and feeling, and a natural sense of the self in the world. All men live in the world, and the world ought to be a place for them to live.[26]

In the *Dutchman,* the victim is Clay. Here Jones shows how black being has become so intertwined with white being that the only possible escape is for black people to kill the "white thing." Apart from this, the only option is to devise means of hiding the true nature of black being, usually through song, dance, poetry, and love. Clay represents a middle-class Negro who is very skilled at hiding his blackness. But in his encounter with Lula and in his attempt to make it with her, he sees himself and tells her the meaning of blackness:

Just let me bleed you, you loud whore, and one poem vanished. A whole people of neurotics, struggling to keep from being sane. And the only thing that would cure the neurosis would be your murder. Simple as that. I mean if I murdered you, then other white people would begin to understand me. You understand? No. I guess not. If Bessie Smith had killed some white people she wouldn't have needed that music. She would have talked very straight and plain about the world. No metaphors. No grunts. No wiggles in the dark of her soul. Just straight two plus two are four. Money, Power, Luxury, like that. All of them. Crazy niggers turning their backs on sanity. When all it needs is that simple act. Murder, Just murder! Would make us all sane.[27]

By killing Clay, Lula demonstrates that white encounter with blackness is threatening to the cultural values of the white West. Therefore the black man has a decision to make. Will he continue to camouflage his creativity, and thus be granted permission to breathe in a white world? Or will he eliminate the "white thing" and by so doing run the risk of being eliminated by it?

A new dimension of liberation is the key to a relevant Black Theology. The Old and the New Testaments are important because in them God is revealed as a God who is involved in history, effecting new forms of human life in the world. Every human order stands under his judgment because only God is absolute. That is why again and again in the Bible a new order is expected which will come into being because of God's decision to make human life really human. This is to say that the Bible is pervasively eschatological; that is, it looks to the future, to a time when the new will displace the old.

Black Theology believes that we are on the threshold of a new order—the order of a new black community. The Black Power movement is a transition in the black community from nonbeing to being. In the old order, black people were not allowed to be human; we were what white America permitted us to be—no-things. We took on false identities which destroyed our real selves, our beautiful black selves. The new order (partially realized now, but not fully consummated) is an order which affirms black self-identity.

VI

Revolution, Violence,
and Reconciliation in Black Theology

> Revolutionary action is a Christian,
> a priestly struggle.
>
> *Camilo Torres*

Because Black Theology is biblical theology seeking to create new value-perspectives for the oppressed, it is revolutionary theology. It is a theology which *confronts* white society as the racist Antichrist, communicating to the oppressor that nothing will be spared in the fight for freedom. It is this attitude which distinguishes it from white American theology and identifies it with the religionists of the Third World. It says with LeRoi Jones:

FACT: There is a racial struggle.

FACT: Any man had better realize what it means. Why there is one. It is the result of more than "misunderstanding." . . .

FACT: "People should love each other" sounds like Riis Park at sundown. It has very little meaning to the world at large.[1]

The debate is over. There will be no more meetings between liberal religious whites and middle-class Negroes to discuss the status of race relations in their communities. Black Theology believes that the problem of racism will not be solved through talk but through *action*. Therefore, its task is to carve out a revolutionary theology based on relevant involvement in the world of racism.

Revolution

The revolution which Black Theology advocates should not be confused with some popular uses of the word. When Billy Graham can speak of a need for a revolution, we clearly require a tighter definition of the term. Revolution is not merely a "change of heart" but a radical black encounter with the structure of white racism, with the full intention of destroying its menacing power. I mean confronting white racists and saying: "If it's a fight you want, I am prepared to oblige you." This is what the black revolution means.

It is important not to confuse protest with revolution. "Revolution is more than protest. Protest merely calls attention to injustice. . . . It is an act of defiance against what is conceived to be an established evil. It is the refusal to be silent in the presence of wrong to which others are accommodated. Social protest flings a gauntlet into the teeth of a suspect authority and challenges the principles upon which that authority claims to rest." [2] It seems that the work of the traditional civil rights organizations falls in this category. Though they changed laws, they were essentially movements which appealed to the conscience of white America. They were asking for black Americans to be included in the total structure of the white American way. Black Power believes that "implicit in the act of protest is the belief that change will be forthcoming once the masters are aware of the protestors' 'grievance' (the very word connotes begging, supplicating to the gods)." [3]

In contrast, "revolution sees every particular wrong as one more instance in a pattern which is itself beyond rectification. Revolution aims at the substitution of a new system for one adjudged to be corrupt, rather than corrective adjustments within the existing system. . . . The power of revolution is coercive." [4] The pre-Civil War black preachers were revolutionary in that they believed that the system itself was evil and consequently urged slaves to rebel against it. The very existence of the black church meant that men like Richard Allen and Absalom Jones were convinced that the evil of racism in the white church was beyond redemption. Today the Black Power movement is an expression of this same revolutionary zeal in the black community. It shuns protest and seeks to speak directly to the needs of the black community. Black Power seeks to change the structure of the black community—its thought forms, values, culture. It tells black people to love themselves, and by so doing, confront white racism with a mode of behavior inimical to everything white.

The revolutionary attitude of Black Theology stems not only from the need of black people to defend themselves in the presence of white oppression, but also from its identity with biblical theology. Like biblical theology, it affirms the absolute sovereignty of God over his creation. This means that ultimate allegiance belongs only to God. Therefore, black people must be taught not to be disturbed about revolution or civil disobedience if the law violates God's purpose for man. The Christian man is obligated by a freedom grounded in the Creator to break all laws which contradict human dignity. Through disobedience to the state, he affirms his allegiance to God as Creator and his willingness to behave as if he believes it. Civil disobedience is a duty in a racist society. That is why Camilo Torres said, "Revolutionary action is a Christian, a priestly struggle." [5]

The biblical emphasis on the freedom of man also means that one cannot allow another to define his existence. If the biblical *imago Dei* means anything, it certainly means that God has created man in such a way that man's own destiny is inseparable from his relation to the Creator. When man denies his freedom and the freedom of others, he denies God. To be for God by responding creatively to the *imago Dei* means that man cannot allow others to make him an It. It is this fact that makes black rebellion human and religious. When black people affirm their freedom in God, they know that they cannot obey laws of oppression. By disobeying, they not only say Yes to God but also to their own humanity and to the humanity of the white oppressor.

Violence

To raise the question of revolution is to raise the question of violence. Revolution always involves coercion. Is Black Theology a theology of violence? Does it advocate guerrilla warfare against the white adversary? These questions are not new. They are the kinds of theoretical questions that we expect from those who sit in the grandstand of middle-class Western morality untouched by the stings of oppression. They are also existential questions which the oppressed themselves are forced to think through as the oppressors continue to tighten the rope. When the oppressed first come to the recognition of their humanity and their treatment as things by the societal structures, the response usually consists of spontaneous, undisciplined outbursts of violence, saying, "We can't stand any more of this." But the masters are always silent on injustice, saying, "Justice will come only in a stable orderly society"—which means at the good pleasure of the white overlords. Therefore, if Black Theology is to speak to the predicament of the oppressed, it must deal honestly with the question of violence.

First, we must realize that to carve out a theology of black revolution which does not sidestep the question of violence is difficult. It is normal, with a Western view of morality, to think that any expression of violence, at least by the disfranchised, is unchristian. By contrast it is quite normal to think that a nation has a right to defend its national interests with violence, especially if it happens to be a part of the "free" world. It is interesting that so many advocates of nonviolence as the only possible Christian response of black people to white domination are also the most ardent defenders of the right of the police to put down black rebellion through violence. Another interesting corollary is their defense of America's right to defend violently the government of South Vietnam against the North. Somehow, I am unable to follow the reasoning.

Our chief difficulty with Black Theology and violence, however, arises from the New Testament itself. The New Testament picture of Jesus seems to suggest that he was against violence as a proper redress. He certainly never resorted to violence. In fact, he seemed to have avoided the term "Messiah" as a personal designation because of its political (violent) implications. Also his constant references to love and the turning of the other cheek seem to indicate that the Christian life cannot be one characterized by an "eye for an eye and a tooth for a tooth." Does not Jesus clearly say that his ministry is for the meek and helpless precisely because they are without an advocate? And even if we agree that love, as suggested in Chapter II, includes power, does this mean the power of violence? Is it not true that the power of love as expressed in the life and death of Jesus eschews the use of violence and emphasizes the inward power of the Christian man to accept everything the enemy dishes out? Is this not what he meant when he said, "Father forgive them, for they know not what they do"? Can we then, by any strength of the imagination or clever exegesis, interpret his command to turn the other cheek to mean a turning of the gun?

These questions are not easy to answer. The real danger of these questions is the implied *literalism* in them. Like the fundamentalist who stressed the verbal inspiration of Scripture, this view suggests that ethical questions dealing with violence can be solved by asking: "What would Jesus do?" We cannot solve ethical questions of the twentieth century by looking at what Jesus did in the first. Our choices are not the same as his. Being Christian does not mean following "in his steps" (remember that book?). His steps are not ours; and thus we are placed in an existential situation in which we are forced to decide without knowing what Jesus would do. The Christian does not ask what Jesus would do, as if Jesus were confined to the first century. He asks: "What is he doing? Where is he at work?" And even though these are the right questions, they cannot be answered once and for all. Each situation has its own problematic circumstances which force the believer to think through each act of obedience without an absolute ethical guide from Jesus. To look for such a guide is to deny the freedom of the Christian man. His only point of reference is the freedom granted in Christ to be all for the neighbor. Therefore, simply to say that Jesus did not use violence is no evidence relevant to the condition of black people as they decide on what to do about white oppression.

"The first task of Christian ethics," writes Bonhoeffer, "is to invalidate this knowledge" (the knowledge of good and evil).[6] Bonhoeffer is referring here to the Pharisaic and philosophical assumption that there is a guide, an absolute standard to right and wrong.

For the Pharisee every moment of life becomes a situation of conflict in which he has to choose between good and evil. For the sake of avoiding any lapse his entire thought is strenuously devoted night and day to the anticipation of the whole immense range of possible conflicts, and to the determination of his own choice.[7]

The Pharisee is a man who figures out on the basis of law what is the right and wrong course of action. If asked why he chose this action rather than that, he can rationally defend himself. Essentially the Pharisee is not a doer of good or evil; he is basically one who judges the actions of others. But to assume that one has knowledge of good and evil is to ignore the fall of man. It assumes that doing the will of God means obeying a system of rules, a pattern of life. It fails, according to Dietrich Bonhoeffer, to recognize that

The knowledge of Jesus is entirely transformed into action, without any reflection upon a man's self. A man's own goodness is now concealed from him. It is not merely that he is no longer obliged to be judge of his own goodness; he must no longer desire to know of it at all; or rather he is no longer permitted to know of it at all. . . . His deed has become entirely unquestioning; he is entirely devoted to his deed and filled with it; his deed is no longer one possibility among many, but the one thing, the important thing, the will of God.[8]

In dealing with the question of violence and black people, Black Theology does not begin by assuming that this question can be answered merely by looking at the Western distinction between right and wrong. It begins by looking at the *face* of black America in the light of Jesus Christ. To be Christian means that one is concerned not about good and evil in the abstract but about men who are lynched, beaten, and denied the basic needs of life. It is not enough to know that black people make up a high percentage of the poor; that white complacency forces them to live in rat-infested apartments; that despite the gains of civil rights laws, police brutality is on the increase; that the appeal to love and nonviolence is a technique of the rich to keep the poor poor. These facts must be translated into human beings. While America is the richest country in the world as a result of the involuntary servitude of blacks and the annihilation of Indians, this country persists in expecting black people to accept their ideals of freedom and democracy. This country expects black people to respect law and order while others beat them over the head. It is this perspective which Black Theology must face before it can deal with the question of violence.

It is not that black Americans suffer more than any other people in the world, or even more than some whites in America. We may even safely assume that the blacks of America suffered more physically in the past than today. As the adversary would say: "Blacks never had it so good." Black suffering is not new. But what is new is "black consciousness." Black people know who they are; and to know who you are is to set limits on your being. It means that any act of oppression will be met with an almighty Halt! Any act of freedom will be met with an almighty

Advance! This is the mood of black America which gives rise to Black Theology.

It does not matter how many gains are made in civil rights. Progress is irrelevant. The face of the black revolutionary will always be there as long as white people persist in defining the boundary of black being. It is the price one pays for oppression. The System, symbolized in the words "law and order," can only mean injustice for black people as long as the structure operates on the basis of racism. The appeal to democracy becomes a façade behind which the white hierarchy defends its right to rule over blacks. In any case the majority of black people see no relationship between the democratic process and their attempt to be free.

It is in this situation that Black Theology must speak the Word of God. How does it begin to deal with the face of the black revolutionary? Black Theology says, with José Bonino, that "A Christian must think through the question of revolution on the basis of his faith and he must express this interpretation in the concrete situation and translate it into action." [9] This means that the Christian is placed in a situation in which he alone makes the choice. The dichotomy between "good and evil," "right and wrong" is a false one. The Christian man

has not to simply decide between right and wrong and between good and evil, but between right and right and between wrong and wrong. . . . Precisely in this respect responsible action is a free venture; it is not justified by any law; it is performed without any claim to a valid self-justification, and therefore also without any claim to an ultimate valid knowledge of good and evil. Good, as what is responsible, is performed in ignorance to good and in surrender to God of the deed which has become necessary and which is nevertheless, or for that very reason, free.[10]

Black Theology realizes that violence per se is not the primary question. Violence is a "subordinate and relative question."

It is subordinate because it has to do with the "cost" of desired change—the question of the legitimacy of revolution is not decided on the basis of the legitimacy of violence and vice versa! Violence is a cost that must be estimated and pondered in relation to a particular revolutionary situation. It is "relative" because in most revolutionary situations . . . violence is already a fact constitutive of the situation: injustice, slave labor, hunger and exploitation are forms of violence which must be weighed against the cost of revolutionary violence.[11]

It is this fact that most whites seem to overlook—the fact that violence already exists. The Christian does not decide between violence and nonviolence, evil and good. He decides between the less and the greater evil. He must ponder whether revolutionary violence is less or more deplorable than the violence perpetuated by the system. There are no absolute rules which can decide the answer with certainty. But he must make a choice. If he decides to take the "nonviolent" way, then he is saying that revolutionary violence is more detrimental to man in the long run than systemic violence. But if the system is evil, then revolutionary violence is both justified and necessary.

Whether the American system is beyond redemption we will have to wait and see. But we can be certain that black patience has run out, and unless white America responds positively to the theory and activity of Black Power, then a bloody, protracted civil war is inevitable. There have occasionally been revolutions —massive redistributions of power—without warfare. It is passionately to be hoped that this can be one of them. The decision lies with white America and not least with white Americans who speak the name of Christ.

Reconciliation

When Black Theology emphasizes the necessity of a theology of revolution based on the unity of black people committed to the task of destroying white racism, it is to be expected that many white religious people will ask: "What about the biblical message of reconciliation?" Whites who ask the question of blacks should not be surprised if some blacks reply: "Yeah man, what about it?" The question, while it may be legitimate, bears a close resemblance to the old (new?) questions about integration and love. White people, creating the barriers of separation, now want to know whether black people are willing to let bygones be bygones. That is why Stokely Carmichael said: "As for separatism what are they talking about? We have no choice. . . . They separated us a long time ago and they sure intend to keep it that way." [12]

White people have short memories. Otherwise, how are black people to interpret questions about reconciliation, love, and other white values? Is it human to expect black people to pretend that their parents were not chattels in society? Do they really expect black people to believe that their status today is unrelated to the slavery of the past? Do they expect black people to believe that this society is not basically racist from top to bottom? And now white religious people want to know what can be done about the "wall of hostility" between blacks and whites. Some critics of Black Theology are certainly going to suggest that my approach to theology will do more toward the separation of black and white Americans than toward reconciliation, and yet there is an appropriate concluding word to be spoken about reconciliation.

First, let me say that reconciliation on white racist terms is impossible, since it would crush the dignity of black people. Under these conditions blacks must treasure their hostility, bringing it fully into consciousness as an irreducible quality of their identity. If white people insist on laying the ground rules for reconciliation, which can only mean black people denying the beauty of their blackness, then black people must do everything within their power to destroy the white thing. Black people can only speak of reconciliation when the black community is permitted to do *its* thing. The black community has experienced the crushing white thing too long. Therefore, Black Theology believes that in order for reconciliation to be meaningful and productive, black people must have room to do their thing. The black community itself must lay down the rules of the game.

White oppressors are incompetent to dictate the terms of reconciliation because they are enslaved by their own racism and will inevitably seek to base the terms on their right to play God in human relationships. The history of slavery and Jim Crow and "integration" efforts renders white people virtually incapable of knowing even how to talk to black people as persons. It is this fact that nullifies the "good" intentions of concerned white religious people who insist that they are prepared to relate to black people as human beings. They simply do not know how. Since racism is inseparable from the history of America, and since practically all white people in this country are taught from birth to treat blacks as things, Black Theology must counsel black people to be suspicious of all whites who want to be "friends" of black people. Therefore, the real question is not whether Black Theology sees reconciliation as an end but, rather, on whose terms we are to be reconciled.

The problem of reconciliation is the oppressor's problem. Being accustomed to defining human relationships between themselves and the slaves on "I-It" terms, they naturally think that they have a monopoly on truth and right behavior. But when the slaves begin to say No to the God-behavior of the masters, the masters are surprised. They are surprised because they thought the slaves were happy. They cannot believe that the hostilities of the slaves stem from anything that the masters themselves have done. But neither can they believe that the unrest in the slave camps is motivated from within the slave community. Therefore, in an attempt to explain the phenomenon of slave hostility, the masters devise tests which will show that most, if not all, people in the society are happy, and the disorders are created by outside agitators who can easily be lumped into one category—Communists. All unhappiness is a lie created and perpetuated by the ungodly Communists who want to destroy the "free" American society. There are usually enough slaves around who have been so crushed by the forces of evil that they do in fact respond according to the intentions of the masters. These slaves become the actual evidence that the slaves as a whole are satisfied with their condition. With this kind of assurance, the masters can begin to stamp out offenders against law and order, killing or caging all who refuse to cooperate with the laws against humanity. It is impossible for the oppressed black people of America to have dialogue with men who have this perspective. They can only say in word and deed: "Think what you like about America and its goodness toward blacks, but the black experience is different. And as long as you persist in that attitude, not only will there be no reconciliation, but soon it will be impossible even for us mutually to survive."

But sometimes it dawns on the liberal oppressors that the oppressed do not wish to be slaves any longer and will stop at nothing to break the chains. Sometimes it enters their minds that "progress" is irrelevant. What the oppressed want is Freedom Now! When the liberal oppressors come to that recognition, they will ask: "What are we to do?" These people want to know whether all has been lost. They are inquiring whether reconciliation is possible in spite of slavery and the present crushing of every black attempt to be black.

What can we say to this group? We must inform them as calmly and clearly as possible that black people cannot talk about the possibilities of reconciliation until full emancipation has become a reality for *all* black people. We cannot talk about living together as brothers (the "black and white together" attitude) as long as they do everything they can to destroy us. While black people may continue to work in the factories, teach in schools, and even fight in wars, there is no law that blacks have to "love" whites. And as long as whites may pass laws against blacks, black people will affirm their dignity in spite of white racism at every opportunity. This country is and will

continue to be two societies—one black and one white—as long
as whites demand the right to define the basis of relationship.
For white people to speak of reconciliation at the very moment
that they are subduing every expression of black self-determination is the height of racist arrogance.

Some of our liberal white friends will probably insist that we
are not being fair. When white people speak of black people
being fair, I am reminded of John O. Killen's Solly Saunders in
And Then We Heard the Thunder. When Solly rejected his
white mistress' love because of his realization that all blacks are
the same to whites, she says: "You hate me because I'm white,
and I don't blame you, but it isn't fair—it just isn't fair." But
Solly replies:

Fairness is a thing no white man has a right to ask of colored.
I mean, look—who's been unfair to whom? Who's been unfair to
my mother and her mother and my father and his father and who'll
be unfair to my son and his children? "Fairness" is a word that
should choke in the white man's throat. I'm not asking any white
man to be fair with Solly Saunders, baby. I live with no such false
illusions.[13]

Do not misunderstand me. Black Theology is a theology which
takes seriously God's reconciling act in Jesus Christ. In fact,
the heart of the New Testament message is the gospel of reconciliation. As St. Paul says: "God was in Christ reconciling the
world to himself" (II Cor. 5:19). Among other things, this
means that the wall of hostility is broken down between blacks
and whites, making color irrelevant to man's essential nature.
But in a white racist society, Black Theology believes that the
biblical doctrine of reconciliation can be made a reality only
when white people are prepared to address black men as *black*
men and not as some grease-painted form of white humanity.
Black Theology will not respond positively to whites who insist
on making blacks as white as possible by de-emphasizing their
blackness and stressing the irrelevance of color while really

living as racists. As long as whites live like *white* people (through marriage, schools, neighborhood, power, etc.) black people must use blackness as the sole criterion for dialogue. Otherwise reconciliation will mean black people living according to white rules and glorifying white values, being orderly and calm while others enact laws which will destroy them.

Black Theology must reject outright this style of behavior and insist that black people can bring something to the relationship. They must bring a system of black values which deny that "white is right" and stress the beauty of being black. They must bring *color* to a sterile and depraved white people who have endeavored to label this world "for white only."

The task of Black Theology is to make the biblical message of reconciliation contemporaneous with the black situation in America. According to the New Testament, reconciliation is the exclusive work of God in which he becomes man in Jesus Christ in order that depraved humanity might become whole. Karl Barth puts it in this way:

The subject-matter, origin and content of the message received and proclaimed by the Christian community is at its heart the free act of the faithfulness of God in which he takes the lost cause of man, who has denied him as Creator and in so doing ruined himself as creature, and makes it his own in Jesus Christ, carrying it through to its goal and in that way maintaining and manifesting his own glory in the world.[14]

Reconciliation means that God has changed the God-man relationship by making the cause of the creature the Creator's cause. The Incarnation means that reconciliation is no longer hoped for but is a reality; it is a reality because God has done for man what man was powerless to do for himself. Basically, this means a restoration of diseased humanity. It means that man can now be what he is—a creature made for fellowship with God.

But that is only one side of reconciliation. To be reconciled with God involves reconciliation with the neighbor. To be pledged to God is to be pledged to other men. That is why the reconciling work of Jesus Christ involves a gathering of those who are committed to obedience in the world. The Christian community is inseparable from the work of the Holy Spirit. It is that community which accepts God's justification of man in Christ and is thus prepared to live as justified men.

When we analyze the black-white relationship in the twentieth century in the light of God's reconciling work in Jesus Christ, the message is clear. For black people it means that God has reconciled us to an acceptance of our blackness. If the death-resurrection of Christ means anything, it means that the blackness of black people is a creation of God himself. God came into the world in order that black people need not be ashamed of who they are. In Christ we not only know who we are, but who God is. This is the heart of the biblical message. God has created man in such a way that man's humanity is inseparable from divine fellowship. Speaking of "the covenant as the presupposition of reconciliation," Barth says:

From the very first God was and is God for man, inclined to him, caring for him, his God. But so, too . . . from the very first man was and is man for God, subordinated and referred to Him. "Ye shall be my people" means that it is proper to you and required of you in your being, life and activity to correspond to the fact that in My being, life and activity for you I am your God.[15]

It is an expression of man's inhumanity to rebel against God. Therefore, when black people say Yes to their humanity by affirming their blackness, we must conclude that the affirmation was made possible through God's reconciling act in Jesus Christ.

The task of Black Theology is to inform black people that because of God's act in Christ they need not offer anyone an apology for being black. Rather, be glad of it! Shout it! It is the purpose for which we were created. This is the meaning of the gospel of reconciliation to black people.

Reconciliation not only means that black people are reconciled to themselves and thus to God, but also to other men. When the other men are white people, this means the black people will bring their new restored image of themselves into every human encounter. They will remain black in their confrontation with others and will demand that others address them as *black* people. They will not let Whitey make an It of them, but will insist, with every ounce of strength, that they are people.

For white people, God's reconciliation in Jesus Christ means that God has made black people a beautiful people; and if they are going to be in relationship with God, they must enter by means of their black brothers, who are a manifestation of God's presence on earth. The assumption that one can know God without knowing blackness is the basic heresy of the white churches. They want God without blackness, Christ without obedience, love without death. What they fail to realize is that in America, God's revelation on earth has always been black, red, or some other shocking shade, but never white. Whiteness, as revealed in the history of America, is the expression of what is wrong with man. It is a symbol of man's depravity. God cannot be white, even though white churches have portrayed him as white. When we look at what whiteness has done to the minds of men in this country, we can see clearly what the New Testament meant when it spoke of the principalities and powers. To speak of Satan and his powers becomes not just a way of speaking but a fact of reality. When we can see a people who are being controlled by an ideology of whiteness, then we know what reconciliation must mean. The coming of Christ means a denial of what we thought we were. It means destroying the white devil in us. Reconciliation to God means that white people are prepared to deny themselves (whiteness), take up the cross (blackness) and follow Christ (black ghetto).

To be sure, this is not easy. But whoever said the gospel of Christ was easy? Obedience always means going where we otherwise would not go; being what we would not be; doing what we would not do. Reconciliation means that Christ has freed us for this. In a white racist society, Christian obedience can only mean being obedient to blackness, its glorification and exaltation.

The problem with white society is that it wants to assume that everything is basically all right. It wants black people to assume that slavery never existed, and the present brutalities inflicted on them are the working of isolated individuals and not basically a part of the system itself. In this sense reconciliation would mean admitting that white values are the values of God. It means black people accepting the white way of life. It assumes that black people have no values except those which are given by the white masters.

But according to Black Theology, it is the other way around. Reconciliation does not transcend color, thus making us all white. The problem of values is not that white people need to instill values in the ghetto; but white society itself needs values so that it will no longer need a ghetto. Black values did not create the ghetto; white values did. Therefore, God's Word of reconciliation means that we can only be justified by becoming black. Reconciliation makes us all black. Through this radical change, we become identified totally with the suffering of the black masses. It is this fact that makes all white churches anti-Christian in their essence. To be Christian is to be one of those whom God has chosen. God has chosen black people!

It is to be expected that many white people will ask: "How can I, a *white* man, become black? My skin is white and there is nothing I can do." Being black in America has very little to do with skin color. To be black means that your heart, your soul, your mind, and your body are where the dispossessed are. We all know that a racist structure will reject and threaten a black man in white skin as quickly as a black man in black skin. It accepts and rewards whites in black skins nearly as well as whites in white skins. Therefore, being reconciled to God does not mean that one's skin is physically black. It essentially depends on the color of your heart, soul, and mind. Some may want to argue that persons with skins physically black will have a running start on others; but there seems to be enough evidence that though one's skin is black, the heart may be lily white. The real questions are: Where is your identity? Where is your being? Does it lie with the oppressed blacks or with the white oppressors? Let us hope that there are enough to answer this question correctly so that America will not be compelled to acknowledge a common humanity only by seeing that blood is always one color.

NOTES

Introduction

1. Kenneth B. Clark, "The Present Dilemma of the Negro" in *The Journal of Negro History,* Vol. LIII (1968), pp. 1–11.
2. Clark, *Dark Ghetto* (New York: Harper Torchbooks, 1965), pp. 79–80. Used with permission.
3. Jones, *Negro Digest,* April, 1965.

Chapter 1: Toward a Constructive Definition of Black Power

1. Richard Wright used the term as early as 1954 in reference to Africa.
2. Camus, *The Rebel,* trans. Anthony Bower (New York: Random House, 1956), p. 13.
3. *Ibid.*
4. *Ibid.,* p. 15. Emphasis added.
5. Most Black Power advocates have dropped the slogan because of its misuse by white liberals.
6. Camus, *The Rebel,* p. 16.
7. Quoted in Floyd B. Barbour (ed.), *The Black Power Revolt* (Boston: Porter Sargent, 1968), p. 39.
8. Tillich, *The Courage to Be* (New Haven: Yale University Press, 1952), p. 3.
9. The word "other," which designates the neighbor, occurs frequently in Franz Fanon, *Black Skins, White Masks,* trans. C. L. Markmann (New York: Grove Press, 1967).
10. Tillich, *The Courage to Be,* p. 66.
11. *Ibid.*
12. Rollo May, *Psychology and the Human Dilemma* (Princeton: Van Nostrand, 1967), p. 73.
13. *Ibid.*
14. Fanon, *Black Skins,* p. 216.
15. *Ibid.,* p. 218.
16. *Ibid.,* p. 131.
17. *Ibid.*
18. *Ibid.,* p. 229.
19. W. R. Mueller and J. Jacobsen, "Samuel Beckett's Long Last Saturday: To Wait or Not to Wait" in Nathan Scott, Jr., *Man in Modern Theatre* (Richmond, Va.: John Knox Press, 1965), p. 77.
20. Quoted in L. H. Fishel, Jr., and Benjamin Quarles, *The Negro American* (Glenview, Ill.: Scott, Foresman and Co., 1967), pp. 204–205. Emphasis added.

21. "Reply to Horace Greeley," 1862, in *The American Tradition in Literature,* Vol. I; revised, S. Bradley, R. C. Beatty, and E. H. Long, eds. (New York: W. W. Norton, 1962), p. 1567.

22. Quoted in Charles Silberman, *Crisis in Black and White* (New York: Random House, 1964), pp. 92–93.

23. See John H. Franklin and Isidore Starr (eds.), *The Negro in Twentieth Century America* (New York: Random House, 1967), pp. 45–46. Here is an analysis by six American historians of how most scholars give a "white" twist to history.

24. A fuller discussion of Christianity and Black Power is found in the next chapter.

25. It should be pointed out here that another alternative for black people is to submit to the white view of blacks. The problem of self-hatred is discussed in this chapter under the heading, "Why Integration Is Not the Answer."

26. Camus, *The Rebel,* p. 17.

27. *Ibid.,* p. 23.

28. Silberman, *Crisis in Black and White,* p. 54.

29. Quoted in Lerone Bennett, *The Negro Mood* (New York: Ballantine Books, 1964), pp. 145–146.

30. James Baldwin, *The Fire Next Time* (New York: The Dial Press, 1963). Used with permission. Quotation is from the Dell paperback, pp. 94–95.

31. Stokely Carmichael and Charles Hamilton, *Black Power: The Politics of Liberation in America* (New York: Random House, 1967), p. 47.

32. In its crudest sense, it means black men want their women. Some psychologists have suggested that every inhuman act of white men toward black men is in part an act of sexual revenge. See Fanon, *Black Skins.*

33. Alvin Poussaint, "The Negro American: His Self-Image and Integration" in Barbour, *The Black Power Revolt,* p. 94.

34. *Ibid.,* p. 96.

35. Fanon, Poussaint, and others agree.

36. Poussaint, in Barbour, *The Black Power Revolt,* p. 95.

37. *Ibid.* p. 99.

38. Wright, *Native Son* (New York: Harper & Row, 1966 ed.), pp. 311–312.

39. Lerone Bennett, *Confrontation: Black and White* (Baltimore: Penguin Books, 1966), pp. 254–255. Used with permission of Johnson Publishing Co., Chicago, the original publishers (copyright © 1965).

40. "Freedom's Journal," March, 1827, quoted in Silberman, *Crisis in Black and White,* p. 189.

41. Leo Tolstoy, quoted in *ibid.,* p. 224.

42. Wright, *Native Son,* p. 395.

43. Bennett, *Confrontation,* p. 256.

44. Fanon, *Black Skins,* p. 85.

45. *Ibid.,* p. 86.

46. *Ibid.*

47. Clark, *Dark Ghetto,* p. 229.

48. Quoted in Fanon, *Black Skins* (Copyright © 1967 by Grove Press), p. 89. Emphasis added. Used with permission.

49. *Ibid.,* pp. 88–89.

50. Quoted in *ibid.,* p. 90. Used with permission.

51. Quoted in *ibid.,* pp. 91–92.

52. Quoted in Francis L. Broderick and August Meier, *Negro Protest Thought in the Twentieth Century* (New York: Bobbs-Merrill Co., 1965), p. 334.

53. For an analysis of John Brown by black writers, see W. E. B. DuBois, *John Brown* (New York: International Publishers, 1962); and Bennett, *Confrontation* and *Negro Mood*.

Chapter 2: The Gospel of Jesus, Black People, and Black Power

1. The most notable exception is Joseph R. Barndt, *Why Black Power?* (New York: Friendship Press, 1968); see also Kyle Haselden's perceptive treatment in *The Racial Problem in Christian Perspective* (New York: Harper & Row, 1959), as well as Liston Pope, *The Kingdom Beyond Caste* (New York: Friendship Press, 1957), and Daisuke Kitagawa, *The Pastor and the Race Issue* (New York: Seabury Press, 1965). Among the best treatments by black theologians see George Kelsey, *Racism and the Christian Understanding of Man* (New York: Charles Scribner's Sons, 1965) and Joseph R. Washington, *The Politics of God* (Boston: Beacon Press, 1967); compare the latter with his *Black Religion* (Boston: Beacon Press, 1964). For an excellent analysis of Black Power and some of its theological implications, see Nathan Wright, Jr., *Black Power and Urban Unrest* (New York: Hawthorn Books, 1967).

2. See Harvey Cox, *God's Revolution and Man's Responsibility* (Valley Forge: Judson Press, 1965) and several excellent essays by other authors in Cox (ed.), *The Church Amid Revolution* (New York: Association Press, 1967), essays prepared for the World Council of Churches' Geneva Conference on Church and Society; see also John C. Bennett, "Christians Look at Revolution," *Christian Century,* February 1, 1967.

3. See Cox (ed.), *Church Amid Revolution,* and the report of the Theological Commission of the (Prague) Christian Peace Conference, October, 1966, in "The Just Revolution," *Frontier,* Spring, 1967.

4. In the future I hope to analyze in more detail the structure of Christian theology from the point of view of oppressed blacks.

5. Maulana Ron Karenga, quoted in Vincent Harding, "The Religion of Black Power," in *The Religious Situation: 1968,* ed. D. R. Cutler (Boston: Beacon Press, 1968), p. 8.

6. *Ibid.,* pp. 28–29.

7. Social scientists, theologians, and others have already shown the destructive nature of racism. Few men would even attempt to reconcile racism and Christianity. See Kelsey, *Racism and the Christian Understanding of Man,* for an excellent theological analysis of the incompatibility.

8. Friedrich Schleiermacher, *The Christian Faith,* trans. J. Baillie (New York: Charles Scribner's Sons, 1922), p. 9.

9. Pannenberg, *Jesus: God and Man,* trans. L. L. Wilkins and D. Priebe (Philadelphia: Westminster Press, 1964), p. 11. Copyright © 1968 by the publisher. Used with permission.

10. *Ibid.,* p. 19.

11. *Ibid.*

12. For support of this translation see Gunther Bornkamm, *Jesus of Nazareth,* trans. Irene and Fraser McLuskey with James Robinson (New York: Harper & Row, 1960), pp. 79, 203 n. 29; and Joachim Jeremias, *The Parables of Jesus,* trans. S. H. Hooke (New York: Charles Scribner's Sons, 1955), p. 100 n. 54.

13. "Toward a Political Hermeneutics of the Gospel," *Union Seminary Quarterly Review*, Vol. XXIII, No. 4 (Summer, 1968), pp. 313–314. Copyright © 1968 by Union Theological Seminary in the City of New York. Used with permission.

14. See Helmut Thielicke, *The Freedom of the Christian Man*, trans. J. W. Doberstein (New York: Harper & Row, 1963), p. 10.

15. *Ibid.*, p. 15.

16. Washington makes this point, drawing a parallel between black people and Israel, a people "chosen" not merely for self-liberation but also for the liberation of her captors; see *The Politics of God*, p. 157.

17. N. H. Snaith, "Righteous, Righteousness," in Alan Richardson (ed.), *A Theological Word Book of the Bible* (New York: Macmillan Co., 1950), p. 203.

18. Barth, *Church Dogmatics*, Vol. I, Part I, trans. T. Parker, W. Johnston, H. Knight, and J. Haire (Edinburgh: T. & T. Clark, 1957), p. 386.

19. *Ibid.* p. 387.

20. Dietrich Bonhoeffer, *The Cost of Discipleship* (New York: Macmillan Co. 1961), p. 158.

21. Barth, *Church Dogmatics*, I/1, p. 387.

22. *Ibid.* Used with permission.

23. Quoted in Vincent Harding, "The Religion of Black Power," in *Religious Situation*, p. 4.

24. *Ibid.*, p. 3.

25. *Ibid.*, p. 6.

26. *Ibid.*, p. 7.

27. The definitive study of Christian love is Anders Nygren, *Agape and Eros*, trans. P. S. Watson (Philadelphia: Westminster Press, 1953).

28. See *ibid.*, pp. 75–81.

29. *Ibid.*, p. 77.

30. *Ibid.*, p. 78.

31. *Ibid.*

32. C. E. B. Cranfield, "Love" in Richardson, *Theological Word Book*, p. 134.

33. Gottfried Quell and Ethelbert Stauffer, "Love," in *Bible Key Words from G. Kittel's Theologisches Wörterbuch zum Neuen Testament*, Vol. I, trans. J. R. Coates (New York: Harper & Row, 1951), p. 45.

34. See Bonhoeffer, *Cost of Discipleship*.

35. Wright, *Black Power*, p. 136.

36. Quoted in Harding, in *Religious Situation*, p. 11.

37. *Ibid.*, p. 5.

38. *Ibid.*, p. 6.

39. Tillich, *Love, Power, and Justice* (New York: Oxford University Press, 1960; a Galaxy Book).

40. *Ibid.*, p. 11.

41. *Ibid.*, p. 25.

42. *Ibid.*, p. 40.

43. *Ibid.*, p. 49.

44. *Ibid.*

45. *Ibid.*, p. 50.

46. "Black Power," a statement by the National Committee of Negro Churchmen, July 31, 1966, quoted in Wright, *Black Power*, p. 187.

47. Schweizer, "Spirit of God," in *Bible Key Words,* Vol. III (1960), p. 2.
48. *Ibid.*
49. Aimé Césaire, quoted in Fanon, *Black Skins,* p. 90.
50. L. Bennett, *Negro Mood,* p. 155, substituting "racism" for the original "slavery," since the two terms are theologically and politically equivalent.
51. *Ibid.*
52. Bornkamm, *Jesus of Nazareth,* p. 111.
53. *Ibid.*
54. Kierkegaard, *Concluding Unscientific Postscript,* trans. D. F. Swenson and W. Lowrie (Princeton: Princeton University Press, 1963), p. 540.
55. *Ibid.*
56. Barth, *Church Dogmatics,* Vol. I, Part 2, trans. G. Bromiley and T. Torrance (Edinburgh: T. & T. Clark, 1956), p. 203.
57. William Hordern, *Speaking of God* (New York: Macmillan Co., 1964), p. 176.

Chapter 3: The White Church and Black Power

1. See their *Black Power: The Politics of Liberation in America.*
2. Some biblical scholars identify the call of Abraham as the beginning of the Church, but this involves critical-historical problems that are not pertinent here. As far as Israel's awareness of herself as an elect people is concerned, few authorities would fail to place the beginning at the exodus and wilderness experiences.
3. For an analysis of the relationship between *qahal* and *ekklesia* see J. Robert Nelson, *The Realm of Redemption* (New York: Seabury Press, 1951), pp. 3–19.
4. Bonhoeffer, *Prisoner for God,* ed. Eberhard Bethge, trans. R. H. Fuller (New York: Macmillan Co., 1953), pp. 166–167. Used with permission.
5. Cox, *The Secular City* (New York: Macmillan Co., 1965), p. 145.
6. Cullmann, *Christ and Time,* trans. F. V. Filson (Philadelphia: Westminster Press, 1949).
7. Lewis, *The Johannine Epistles* (London: Epworth Press, 1961), p. 84.
8. *Ibid.*
9. Hordern, *Christianity, Communism and History* (London: Lutterworth Press, 1957), p. 27.
10. Quoted in Cox, *Secular City,* p. 126.
11. *Ibid.,* p. 144.
12. Barth, *Church Dogmatics,* Vol. IV, Part 1, trans. G. Bromiley (Edinburgh: T. & T. Clark, 1956), p. 643.
13. *Ibid.,* p. 695.
14. *Ibid.,* p. 696.
15. Haselden, *The Racial Problem,* p. 48.
16. *Ibid.*
17. Berton, *The Comfortable Pew* (Philadelphia: J. B. Lippincott Co., 1965), pp. 28–29.
18. Loescher, *The Protestant Church and the Negro, a Pattern of Segregation* (New York: Association Press, 1948), p. 9.
19. Haselden, *The Racial Problem,* p. 29.
20. *Ibid.*
21. E. Franklin Frazier, *Black Bourgeoisie* (New York: Collier Books, 1965), p. 115. Used with permission.

22. Quoted in *ibid.*, p. 115.

23. *Ibid.*

24. See Washington, *Black Religion* and *Politics of God;* H. Richard Niebuhr, *The Social Sources of Denominationalism* (Cleveland: Meridian Books, 1929); Haselden, *The Racial Problem;* E. Franklin Frazier, *The Negro Church in America* (New York: Schocken Books, 1963).

25. Quoted in Niebuhr, *Social Sources of Denominationalism,* p. 249.

26. *Ibid.*, p. 251.

27. *Ibid.*, p. 260.

28. *Ibid.*, p. 244.

29. *Ibid.*, pp. 247–248.

30. Shelton Smith, Robert Handy, and Lefferts Loetscher, *American Christianity,* Vol. I (New York: Charles Scribner's Sons, 1960), p. 181.

31. See Ralph Ginzburg, *One Hundred Years of Lynching* (New York: Lancer Books, 1962).

32. Myrdal, *An American Dilemma: The Negro Problem and Modern Democracy* (New York: Harper & Brothers, 1944), p. 563.

33. Haselden, *The Racial Problem,* p. 63. Used with permission.

34. Bornkamm, *Jesus of Nazareth,* p. 82.

35. Harding, "The Religion of Black Power," in *Religious Situation,* p. 12.

36. Barth, *Church Dogmatics,* Vol. I, Part 1, p. 1.

37. *Ibid.*, p. 3.

38. Tillich, *Systematic Theology,* Vol. I (Chicago: University of Chicago Press, 1951).

39. J. Washington, *Black Religion,* p. 228.

Chapter 4: The Black Church and Black Power

1. Howard Thurman, *The Negro Spiritual Speaks of Life and Death* (New York: Harper & Row, 1947), pp. 13–14.

2. Myrdal, *American Dilemma,* p. 860.

3. Allen, *The Life, Experience, and Gospel Labors of the Right Reverend Richard Allen* (Philadelphia: A.M.E. Book Concern), p. 5.

4. Benjamin E. Mays and J. W. Nicholson, *The Negro's Church* (New York: Institute of Social Research, 1933), p. 3.

5. Quoted in Mays, *The Negro's God* (Boston: Chapman and Grimes, 1938), p. 46.

6. Quoted in *ibid.*, p. 42.

7. *Ibid.*, pp. 43–44.

8. *Ibid.*, p. 44.

9. *Ibid.*, p. 49.

10. Quoted in Paul M. Van Buren, *The Secular Meaning of the Gospel* (New York: Macmillan Co., 1963). See also Bonhoeffer, *Letters and Papers from Prison,* revised, trans. R. Fuller, Frank Clarke, and others (New York: Macmillan Co., 1967), p. 188.

11. Quoted in Mays, *Negro's God,* p. 49.

12. "Bishop Daniel Alexander Payne's Protestation of American Slavery," *Journal of Negro History,* Vol. LII (1967), p. 60.

13. Washington, *Black Religion,* p. 202.

14. Moltmann, *Theology of Hope,* trans. J. W. Leitch (New York: Harper & Row, 1967), p. 21; there is a remarkable correlation between Moltmann's viewpoint on Christian hope and the perspective of the slave preachers.

15. *Ibid.*

16. *Ibid.,* p. 33.

17. *Ibid.,* p. 100. Moltmann is here describing the role of the promise of God in the life of Israel, a description that seems strikingly appropriate to the situation of black people.

18. Mays and Nicholson, *Negro's Church;* Washington, *Black Religion.*

19. It is interesting to note that Washington seems to have reversed his perspective in his more recent *Politics of God,* where black folk religion is described as authentic Christianity and black people are described as God's chosen people.

20. Mays and Nicholson, *Negro's Church,* p. 30.

21. Washington, *Black Religion,* p. 35.

22. St. Clair Drake and Horace R. Cayton, *Black Metropolis,* Vol. II (New York: Harper & Row, 1962), p. 420.

23. *Ibid.*

24. Mays and Nicholson, *Negro's Church,* p. 7.

25. One important exception was the Abyssinian Baptist Church and its minister, Adam Clayton Powell, Jr. During the early 1940's he recognized the meaning of the gospel and its perversion by white churches. "The great wedge that keeps America split is the hypocrisy of the Christian Church. The fundamental postulate of Christianity is equality and brotherhood. We have perverted this glorious doctrine to exclude interracial love. Religion has lost its ethical integrity and there, its moral dynamic" (*Marching Blacks: An Interpretative History of the Rise of the Black Common Man* [New York: Dial Press, 1945], p. 95).

26. "Findings of Black Methodists for Church Renewal" (Cincinnati: Service Center of the Board of Missions, United Methodist Church, 1968), pp. 3–4.

27. *Ibid.,* pp. 4–5.

28. "A Statement by the National Committee of Negro Churchmen," *New York Times,* July 31, 1966.

29. This failure is probably due to the early confusion regarding the meaning of the term.

30. Washington, *Politics of God,* p. 209.

Chapter 5: Some Perspectives of Black Theology

1. R. N. Flew and R. E. Davies (eds.), *The Catholicity of Protestantism* (London: Lutterworth Press, 1950), pp. 115–116. This book is a report presented to the Archbishop of Canterbury by a group of Free Churchmen regarding the nature of the Protestant tradition.

2. See William Hordern, *Layman's Guide to Protestant Theology* (New York: Macmillan Co., 1968) for an excellent discussion of these three major developments in Protestant theology. For a discussion by the men who represent these schools, see Harold DeWolf, *The Case for Theology in Liberal Perspective* (Philadelphia: Westminster Press, 1959); William Hordern, *The Case for a New Reformation Theology* (Philadelphia: Westminster Press, 1959); Edward Carnell, *The Case for Orthodox Theology* (Philadelphia: Westminster Press, 1959).

3. B. B. Warfield, *The Inspiration and Authority of the Bible* (Nutley, N. J.: Presbyterian & Reformed, 1948), p. 422.

4. Flew and Davies, *Catholicity*, p. 115.

5. Washington, *Black Religion*, pp. 102–103. Copyright © 1964 by the author. Used with permission of the publisher.

6. Quoted in Gordon Parks, "Stokely Carmichael," *Life*, May 19, 1967, p. 82.

7. Camus, *The Plague*, trans. by Stuart Gilbert (New York: Modern Library, 1948), pp. 196–197. Used with permission.

8. Millar Burrows, *An Outline of Biblical Theology* (Philadelphia: Westminster Press, 1946), p. 181.

9. Moltmann, *Theology of Hope*, p. 329.

10. *Ibid.*, pp. 334–335.

11. *Ibid.*, p. 335.

12. Walter Kaufmann (ed.), *The Portable Nietzsche* (New York: Viking Press, 1954), pp. 611–612. Used with permission.

13. *Ibid.*, p. 612.

14. *Ibid.*, p. 96.

15. Malcolm Boyd, "The Underground Church," *Commonweal*, April 12, 1968, p. 98.

16. *Ibid.*, p. 99. Used with permission.

17. *Ibid.*

18. *Ibid.*, p. 100.

19. Quoted in Barbour, *Black Power Revolt*, p. 122.

20. *Ibid.*, p. 122.

21. Quoted in *ibid.*, p. 165.

22. *Ibid.*

23. *Ibid.*, p. 166.

24. Neal, "The Black Arts Movement," *Black Theatre:* The Drama Review, Vol. 12, No. 4 (T40), Summer, 1968, p. 30. Copyright © 1968 by the publisher. Used with permission.

25. *Ibid.*

26. LeRoi Jones, *Home: Social Essays* (New York: William Morrow, 1966), p. 213. Originally appeared in an article, "The Revolutionary Theatre," in *Liberator* magazine, Vol. V, No. 7 (July, 1965). Used with permission.

27. LeRoi Jones, *Dutchman* and *The Slave* (New York: William Morrow, 1964), p. 35. Copyright © 1964 by the author. Used with permission of the Sterling Lord Agency.

Chapter 6: *Revolution, Violence, and Reconciliation in Black Theology*

1. LeRoi Jones, *Home*, p. 119. Copyright © 1963, 1966, by the author. Used with permission of the publisher.

2. C. Eric Lincoln, "The Black Revolution in Cultural Perspective," *Union Seminary Quarterly Review*, Vol. XXIII, No. 3 (Spring, 1968), p. 221. I am not in total agreement with Lincoln's examples of revolution and protest.

3. Quoted in Neal, *Black Theatre*, p. 30.

4. Lincoln, "Black Revolution," *Union Seminary Quarterly Review*, p. 221–222.

5. Quoted in José M. Bonino, "Christians and the Political Revolution," *The Development Apocalypse*, special U.S. edition of *Risk* edited by Stephen Rose and Peter Vav Lelyveld (1967), p. 109.

6. Bonhoeffer, *Ethics*, edited by Eberhard Bethge and trans. by N. H. Smith (New York: Macmillan Co., 1955), p. 17.

7. *Ibid.*, p. 27. Used with permission.

8. *Ibid.*, pp. 34–35. Used with permission.

9. Bonino, *op. cit.*, pp. 114–115.

10. Bonhoeffer, *Ethics,* p. 249. Used with permission.

11. Bonino, *op. cit.*, p. 116. Used with permission.

12. Quoted in Parks, "Stokely Carmichael," *Life,* May 19, 1967, p. 82.

13. John O. Killen, *And Then We Heard the Thunder* (New York: Pocket Books, 1963), p. 413. Used with permission.

14. Barth, *Church Dogmatics,* IV/1, p. 3. Used with permission.

15. *Ibid.*, p. 42. Used with permission.

Index